Preparing Literature Reviews

Qualitative and Quantitative Approaches

M. Ling Pan

Pyrczak Publishing

P.O. Box 39731 • Los Angeles, CA 90039

Although the author and publisher have made every effort to ensure the accuracy and completeness of information contained in this book, we assume no responsibility for errors, inaccuracies, omissions, or any inconsistency herein. Any slights of people, places, or organizations are unintentional.

Project Director: Monica Lopez.

Cover design by Robert Kibler and Larry Nichols.

Editorial assistance provided by Sharon Young, Brenda Koplin, Kenneth Ornburn, Randall R. Bruce, Cheryl Alcorn, Erica Simmons, and Grace Bell Killorin.

Printed in the United States of America.

ISBN 1-884585-27-2

Contents

Introduction

A literature review is an original work based on a critical examination of the literature on a topic. The reviewer should evaluate the available evidence as well as relevant theories (while noting gaps in the literature) and create a synthesis that points readers in the direction of what seems *likely* to be true about the topic. Reviewers deal with *likelihoods* because all methods of inquiry are subject to error.

Preparing an adequate literature review is far from being a mechanical process; instead, it is part *science* and part *art*. "Science" comes into play because there are usually a considerable number of original research reports to be evaluated when preparing a review. Knowing the basics of the scientific method, many of which are covered in this book, is important to making proper evaluations of relevant research. The "artistic" (i.e., subjective part) comes into play because the reviewer needs to make sense of the *body of literature*, which may require inferential leaps and subjective judgments regarding which sources to emphasize, how to combine various sources, and how to account for gaps in knowledge on a topic so that a cohesive synthesis of the literature results.

Qualitatively Oriented versus Quantitatively Oriented Reviews

As you know from the subtitle of this book, you will learn the basics for preparing both qualitative (i.e., narrative) and quantitative reviews. These do not constitute a dichotomy. Rather, literature reviews exist on a continuum from very highly *qualitative* (with little mention of statistics or the research methods used to obtain them) to very highly *quantitative* (with the final synthesis based on the mathematical averaging of results across various studies reported by different researchers). Most beginning students should consider writing a qualitative review in which statistical material is very judiciously selected for inclusion in the review. This book shows you how to select and interpret such statistical material and how to present it without overwhelming your readers.

As you will learn in this book, qualitative reviews and quantitative reviews have a great deal in common, so almost all of this book (Chapters 1 through 10) will be relevant regardless of the reviewer's orientation to the issue of quantification. Even Chapter 11, which covers the highly quantitative technique called "meta-analysis," contains suggestions for those who write *qualitative* reviews.

About the End-of-Chapter Exercises

The end-of-chapter exercises are designed to be used as homework assignments. They will help you review the material you have read and also, I hope, help you consider how to use what you have learned from each chapter while you are preparing your literature review.

About the Appendices

Appendix A presents a checklist of the guidelines presented throughout this book. It can be used in several ways. First, it serves as an index to help you quickly locate material that you read earlier and want to locate in order to reread and review it. Second, you can use it as a checklist of reminders to reconsider as you write and revise each draft of your review. Third, instructors can use it for easy reference when commenting on students' literature reviews. For instance, instead of writing out a criticism (either positive or negative), an instructor can refer to the checklist to quickly locate appropriate guidelines in order to write statements such as "Please improve this section. See Guideline 8.5." or "Good application of Guideline 9.2."

Appendix B provides an overview of the differences between qualitative and quantitative *research*. In the body of this book, you will find extensive discussions of the differences between qualitative and quantitative *literature reviews*. It is important to note that *research* also can be qualitatively or quantitatively oriented. Appendix B will help you understand the strengths and weaknesses of both orientations to research, which will help you evaluate each type properly when you prepare a literature review.

About the Model Literature Reviews

Three model literature reviews are presented near the end of this book.

They are "models" in the sense that they are well-written examples that illustrate various ways to consider, evaluate, and synthesize literature. Note, however, that no one model fits all purposes. For instance, a literature review written for inclusion in a doctoral dissertation normally would be more extensive and detailed than one written as a senior project by an undergraduate.

The first model review originally appeared as the introduction to a report of original research in a journal article. The remaining two are "stand-alone" literature reviews that were originally published as such—not as introductions to some larger work. The three model literature reviews illustrate varying degrees of quantification, with the last one illustrating the use of meta-analysis, which produces a highly quantified literature review. Even those who plan to write highly *qualitatively* oriented reviews will find techniques in this meta-analysis that might be used when writing literature reviews.

A common set of questions appears at the end of all the model literature reviews. These are designed to help you consider the strengths of each review and will be useful as classroom discussion items.

Concluding Notes

I wish you success in preparing your literature review, and I hope that the guidelines and examples in this book will prove helpful. The guidelines are based on my extensive reading of literature reviews in a variety of fields for more than three decades. I believe that they are firmly in the mainstream of thought on how to prepare literature reviews in the social and behavioral sciences and related fields.

Note that I have included a large number of examples to illustrate the guidelines in this book. The examples that have references, of course, are quoted from published sources (as well as one personal communication). The remaining examples were written by me. In all cases, I wrote examples that parallel types of material I have frequently encountered in literature reviews. In many of these cases, the examples illustrate undesirable techniques that you should avoid. Instead of quoting examples of these (and potentially embarrassing the authors), I created ones similar to those that I have seen in recent literature reviews.

I encourage you to share with me your criticisms of this book so that I can improve it in future editions. You can communicate with me via my publisher. The mailing address is shown on the title page of this book. Also, you can send e-mails to me in care of the publisher at info@pyrczak.com, if you prefer.

M. Ling Pan
Los Angeles, California

Notes

Chapter 1

Qualitative versus Quantitative Reviews

A literature review is a *synthesis* of the literature on a topic. The process of synthesizing involves interpreting, evaluating, and integrating individual pieces of literature to create a new, original written work. In Box 1A is the definition of "synthesis" given in the on-line version of the *Merriam-Webster Unabridged Dictionary* (2002).

Box 1A *Dictionary definition of synthesis.*

> *Synthesis*: "The combining of often varied and diverse ideas, forces, or factors into one coherent or consistent complex."

In light of the definition of the term "synthesis," it is clear that a simple string of summaries of the works of others is a product that should *not* be called a "literature review."

The term *literature* usually refers to written works that have been published either on paper or electronically. For the purposes of this book, however, we will also include personal communications—whether written or oral—as appropriate sources for literature reviews. For example, statements made during an interview with an expert or the answer given to a question posed to the author of a published research report might make valuable contributions to understanding a topic. Of course, the source and date of any personal communications used in a review must be cited. Because they are not published sources, personal communications typically should be used very sparingly.

Brief Overview of Steps in Preparing a Literature Review

The first step is to *select a topic*. In most cases, this is an interactive process in which the initial search of the literature reveals how much exists on a topic. Based on this, the topic may need to be narrowed if there is too much literature or broadened if there is too little. At the same time, the needs of the audience for whom the review is being written will influence the selection of a topic.

The next step is to read the literature and make notes, with an eye toward getting a broad overview of which issues have been thoroughly covered, which ones need more investigation, which principles seem most firmly established and/or most widely accepted as being valid, and, perhaps most important, which theory or theories have a bearing on your topic.

The next steps are to evaluate and interpret the literature. Many authors of literature reviews give high evaluations to sources that present the results of rigorous scientific studies. (Often, these authors *tend* to be quantitatively oriented.) Others give high evaluations to studies that provide crucial insights even if the underlying methods for collecting data are mildly, or even seriously, flawed. (Often, these authors *tend* to be qualitatively oriented.) All authors of literature reviews should pay special attention to literature that presents, tests, and/or builds on theories related to their topics.

Next, the literature needs to be synthesized. This is done by first grouping various sources according to their similarities and differences while considering possible explanations for differences (and contradictions) in the literature. Note that a synthesis very often will not consist of a single, straightforward conclusion. Instead, it might consist of speculation on how the pieces of evidence found in the literature fit together along with some tentative conclusions and their implications. This should lead to suggestions for future research that might produce a more definitive understanding of the topic.

Finally, the first draft of a literature review should be reviewed by others. Of course, a review by an expert is highly desirable. However, note that a well-written review should be comprehensible to even nonexperts such as students who are just beginning their study of an academic area.

Revising (and, in some cases, entirely rewriting) a review in light of the feedback is a crucial step in producing a literature review of high quality.

Box 1B *Summary of major steps in preparing a literature review.*

The major steps are:

1. Select a topic, and modify the topic in light of the amount of available literature and your audience's needs.
2. Read the selected literature carefully in order to get a broad overview, with attention to the relationship of the literature to theory or theories.
3. Evaluate and interpret the literature on the topic.
4. Create a synthesis by reconciling similarities and differences in the literature. Consider the implications of possible conclusions, and identify fruitful areas for future research.
5. Write a first draft, get feedback on it from others, and revise and/or rewrite your review.

Creating a synthesis for a *qualitatively oriented* literature review is more subjective than creating one for a *quantitatively oriented* review. In this book, we will consider both types of reviews.

✤ Guideline 1.1
In quantitatively oriented literature reviews, precise statistical results from the literature are presented and sometimes mathematically combined.

Authors of both quantitative and qualitative reviews should write narratives that describe the importance of their topics, provide overviews of the types of literature that exist on their topics (including gaps in the literature), and make overall evaluations of the bodies of literature on their topics. The main distinction between the quantitatively oriented and qualitatively oriented reviews lies in the extent to which specific statistics are presented and used in creating a synthesis. Those who write quantitatively oriented reviews base their synthesis and conclusions more closely on specific statistical values than those who write qualitatively oriented reviews. Compare the statement in Example 1.1.1 below with the one in Example 1.3.1 (under Guideline 1.3) to get a better understanding of the distinction. Both statements refer to the same three studies.

Example 1.1.1

Sample statement that might appear in a quantitatively oriented review:

The three experiments in which Drug A was compared with a placebo yielded mean reductions on the Pain Relief Scale of 2.1, 3.3, and 4.0 points on a scale from 0 (no pain) to 20 (extreme pain). All three were statistically significant at the $p < .05$ level. The mean (i.e., arithmetic average) of these three means is 3.1, which is our best estimate of the effectiveness of Drug A. Hence, Drug A appears to produce a small but significant reduction in pain.[1]

ꙮ Guideline 1.2

If the main thrust of a review is the mathematical combination of results of various studies by various researchers, the result is called a meta-analysis or meta-analytic review.

The prefix "meta-" means *going beyond* or *transcending*. Thus, meta-analysis refers to a statistical analysis that goes beyond or transcends previous statistical analyses. For example, the author of Example 1.1.1 used a meta-analytic *technique* by going beyond the original analyses and averaging results across three studies.

The use of meta-analytic techniques (such as averaging means or correlation coefficients across studies) is most likely to be found in quantitatively oriented reviews. There is no reason, however, why the author of a primarily qualitatively oriented review could not occasionally use such a

---

[1] As you probably know, the *mean* is the most popular average. When different studies have different numbers of participants (or subjects), a weighting procedure should be employed in getting the mean of the means. This procedure is covered in Chapter 11. For the purposes of this example, we will assume that all three experiments had the same number of participants. Combining statistical results across experiments, as illustrated in Example 1.1.1, is called *meta-analysis*, which is the topic of Chapter 11.

technique to make his or her review more quantitatively oriented than it otherwise would be.

When the main thrust of a review is to identify and include only those studies that lend themselves to statistical averaging and when the synthesis and conclusions are based primarily on this mathematical combination of the statistical results reported by other researchers, the entire document is called a "meta-analysis" or "meta-analytic review."[2]

Chapter 11 describes some straightforward meta-analytic techniques that can be used by those who write *both* quantitatively oriented and qualitatively oriented reviews. In addition, the chapter provides enough information so that one could produce a basic meta-analytic review.

↳ Guideline 1.3
In qualitatively oriented reviews, statistical studies are often described in general terms, but precise statistical values are de-emphasized.

Authors of qualitatively oriented reviews typically present evidence found in the literature with little emphasis on the precise statistical results. Nevertheless, relevant statistical evidence is referred to and even interpreted in a general sense, as illustrated in Example 1.3.1 in which no statistics are reported.

Example 1.3.1
Sample statement that might appear in a qualitatively oriented review:

In each of the three experiments in which Drug A was compared with a placebo, there was a very small but significant reduction in pain reported by those who took the drug. The failure to obtain a large reduction in pain

---

[2] Note that while some researchers regard a meta-analysis as a mathematical literature review, others regard it as original research. Hence, it is not uncommon to find meta-analyses published as original research reports in journals that have editorial policies that do not permit publication of qualitatively oriented or even quantitatively oriented reviews unless they emphasize the creation and interpretation of mathematical syntheses. Also note that if your ultimate goal is publication of your literature review in a journal, you should examine a number of articles in journals to which you might want to submit your review. While some prestigious journals such as *Psychological Bulletin* are mainly devoted to literature reviews, others mainly publish reports in which literature reviews are the preface to reports of original empirical research (see Guideline 1.6 for a definition of "empirical research").

points to the need to investigate other drugs that may be more beneficial in reducing pain.

In summary, authors of highly qualitatively oriented reviews often make very general references to statistical findings but typically report few statistical values.

᭰ Guideline 1.4
Both types of reviews have many common features.

The authors of both qualitatively oriented and quantitatively oriented reviews have an obligation to cover certain common ground, including the following:

a. introducing the topic and defining key terms,
b. establishing the importance of the topic,
c. providing an overview of the amount of available literature and its types (e.g., theoretical, statistical, speculative),
d. describing how they searched for relevant literature,
e. discussing their selection of literature to include in their review (especially if there is much literature on the topic),
f. pointing out gaps in the literature (i.e., areas that are not covered by the literature),
g. describing and, if possible, reconciling discrepancies in the literature,
h. arriving at a synthesis, and
i. discussing possible implications and directions for future research.

These and many other important issues in the preparation of both qualitatively oriented and quantitatively oriented literature reviews are covered in Chapters 2 through 10. Chapter 11 presents meta-analytic techniques, some of which might also be used by those who are preparing qualitatively oriented reviews.

♄ Guideline 1.5

Many literature reviews are a blend of qualitatively oriented and quantitatively oriented approaches.

Many literature reviews employ a blend of techniques. That is why the term "oriented" is used throughout this book. It would be difficult to find in print a purely qualitative review (one without even some general references to statistical results) or to find a purely quantitative review (one without a qualitative narrative component that helps readers interpret the literature in light of the statistical results being reported).

♄ Guideline 1.6

Distinguish between qualitative and quantitative *literature reviews* and qualitative and quantitative *empirical research*.

As you know, a literature review is a narrative essay in which the literature on a topic is evaluated, described, and synthesized. The synthesis may be based on ordering and comparing pieces of literature and using logic (and sometimes, just plain common sense) to arrive at conclusions; such a review is a *qualitatively oriented review*. If the synthesis is based primarily on statistics reported in the literature, it is a *quantitatively oriented review*. In a highly quantitative review (called a "meta-analysis"), statistics from various studies are mathematically combined to create new statistics on which the synthesis is primarily based.

Note that conducting *library research* is *not* equivalent to conducting *empirical research*. The term *empirical* refers to making observations. When it is combined with the term *research*, it refers to a research process in which direct, original observations are made in order to create new data or information. For example, if you select a sample of students enrolled in a college and ask them a series of questions about their satisfaction with the abilities of their instructors, you are generating new data. The data can be in the form of statistics (such as the percentage who answered each yes–no question in a certain way), which is called *quantitative empirical research*. The data for such a study can also be in the form of words that describe students' extended verbal responses to interview questions. These results are often expressed as themes that are typically illustrated with quotations from the participants. This type of empirical research is called *qualitative empirical research*. For more information on the distinctions between qualitative and quantitative empirical research, see Appendix B.

An important implication of this guideline is that the type of literature that exists on a topic may influence the type of review that is written. If most of the literature on a topic consists of reports of qualitative research, a qualitatively oriented review (or at least a blend with an emphasis on qualitative aspects) would be in order. The opposite is true for areas in which most of the research is quantitative.

✎ Guideline 1.7
Read both qualitatively oriented and quantitatively oriented reviews in preparation for writing a review.

One of the best ways to learn how to write in any genre is to read many examples of it. Whether you plan to write a qualitatively oriented or a quantitatively oriented review, make a point of reading at least several examples of each very early in your planning stages. Those of you who feel secure in your knowledge of statistics and prefer a *quantitative* approach to acquiring knowledge might be impressed with how informative and helpful a *qualitative* review can be. On the other hand, those who are qualitatively oriented might find useful techniques to use in a qualitative review by reading quantitative reviews. In this book, we will consider some simple techniques for introducing quantitative information into qualitative reviews.

A good place to start is to read Model Literature Review 1, which is an example of a short, qualitatively oriented review. Note that Model Literature Review 3 is an example of a highly quantitatively oriented review. (The model literature reviews are near the end of this book.)

Note that these model reviews are, in my opinion, good, solid examples, even though they may have characteristics that might be criticized. Also note that a review for one purpose and/or audience might be considered a model of excellence while for another purpose and/or audience, it might be considered quite inadequate. For example, a review that is part of a doctoral thesis or one that is written for possible publication in a top-flight journal normally would be more comprehensive and insightful than one written in a single semester as a term paper for a course. If your primary audience is your professor (or a committee of professors), you should seek their guidance on their expectations for your review—including the issue of whether they would prefer a qualitatively oriented or quantitatively oriented review.

Box 1C *The value of reading literature reviews written by others.*

> Reading sample literature reviews is one of the most important things you can do in order to learn how to write a good review. The more time you have, the more samples you should read before preparing your own review.

Timeline Considerations

Determine how much time is available before the final draft of your literature review is due, and prepare a *written* timeline. Begin by allocating about one-fifth of your available time to each of the five steps in Box 1B. For example, in a ten-week quarter, allocate two weeks for the first step, two weeks for the second, and so on. If a step takes more or less time than initially allocated, revise and *rewrite* your timeline. Putting it in writing will encourage you to start early and pace yourself.

Exercise for Chapter 1

1. A classmate asks you to critique the first draft of a literature review she has written for a class assignment. While reading the draft, you realize that she has, for the most part, simply summarized one study after another—each summarized in its own paragraph. Based on the information in this chapter, what advice would you give her?

2. A classmate tells you she has been assigned to write a literature review that *synthesizes* the literature on a topic. She asks if you know what this means. In your own words, how would you define a "synthesis"?

3. According to this chapter, it is acceptable to cite personal communications in a literature review. Do you agree? Why? Why not?

4. In this chapter, the process of selecting a topic is referred to as "interactive." What elements interact in this process?

5. While some reviewers give high evaluations to literature that reports the results of scientific studies, others may give high evaluations to literature that provides crucial insights even if the scientific methodology is flawed. According to this chapter, to what should all authors of literature reviews pay special attention?

6. In this chapter, what is referred to as a "crucial step" in producing a literature review of high quality?

7. An entire review is called a meta-analysis (i.e., meta-analytic review) when the *main thrust* of the review is to do what?

8. Why is the term "oriented" used throughout this chapter?

9. Briefly define the term "empirical research."

10. To what extent do you agree with this statement, which appears in Box 1C: "Reading sample literature reviews is one of the most important things you can do in order to learn how to write a good review." Do you have any anecdotal evidence (e.g., personal experiences) that help support or refute the statement? Explain.

11. Initially, about how much time should be allocated to each of the five steps named in Box 1B? Is it acceptable to revise your timeline? Explain.

12. *A question for students who have previously written a literature review and/or those who have read reviews extensively*: Do you think that it is possible for a reviewer to be entirely objective? To be very close to being entirely objective? To what extent do statistics help reviewers be objective? Explain.

Chapter 2

Selecting a Topic for Review

The selection of a topic for review is the single most important step in preparing a literature review. This chapter will help you select topics you might want to review. In the next chapter, you will learn how to refine your topic selections.

Box 2A *The importance of topic selection.*

> The selection of a topic for review is the single most important step in preparing a literature review.

✺ Guideline 2.1

Consider carefully your audience's expectations and/or requirements when selecting a topic.

If your primary audience is your professor (or committee of professors), read carefully any handouts on a literature review assignment, and make careful notes of oral directions that are given. If you are not clear on the expectations and requirements, ask for clarification as soon as possible.

Some professors will indicate a fairly short maximum page length and number of references to be cited. For such an assignment, a rather narrow topic is usually desirable so that the literature review will be more than just a superficial overview of a broad area.

Other professors expect students to write as many pages and cite as many references as needed to provide comprehensive reviews of their topics. In this case, a narrow topic will produce a short paper, and a broader topic will provide you with the opportunity to write a long review. In all cases, you should consult with your professor regarding your topic selection very early in the process.

If you are writing for possible publication in a journal, study examples of reviews in journals to which you might submit your review. Often, journals will have guidelines for submission. Sometimes, additional information on content and style is available for specific journals.

✤ Guideline 2.2
When selecting a topic, emphasize your audience's expectations and requirements instead of your personal interests.

Whenever possible, you should write on a topic of interest to you. Some of you may even have a burning desire to write a review on a particular topic. This is acceptable as long as you can approach the topic with an open mind and evaluate fairly any literature that is inconsistent with your theories or opinions on the topic.

It is usually highly undesirable to "force a topic to fit" an assignment. For instance, if you are writing a literature review for a history of sociology course, but you have a strong interest in a new topic that has a very short history, you should put your topic idea aside (for possible use in another course) and select one that is appropriate for the course in which you are currently enrolled.

One reason that submissions to journals are rejected is that they are "off topic." If the editor sees that the topic of your literature review is not within the content domain to which the journal is devoted, your literature review will be returned to you without consideration by the editor's editorial board, which provides advice on which submissions to accept for publication. Journals vary greatly in the types of content they cover. If your goal is publication, make sure that your topic is appropriate for publication in at least two or three journals. Also, note that many academic journals have a policy of not publishing (or seldom publishing) stand-alone literature reviews; that is, they publish exclusively original reports of empirical research that begin with a literature review. For a sample review of this type, examine Model Literature Review 1 in this book.

✍ Guideline 2.3

Put possible topics *in writing*. If your professor is your audience, ask him or her to examine your written topic ideas.

Your topic ideas might be single words, or they may be expressed in short phrases, sentences, or paragraphs. In any case, your ideas should be put in writing. It is often helpful to put your written topic ideas away for a day or two and then reconsider them.

Unless your professor asks you to do otherwise, keep your initial written list of topics simple. Avoid the temptation to write essays about your experiences relating to your potential topics and why you want to learn more about them. Your professor will let you know if and when this type of material should be written.

Presenting topic ideas in writing to your professor will help you avoid miscommunication. The feedback you get from a professor (or a committee of professors) on your topic ideas should not be construed to be a "contract." Like you, your professor may have second thoughts during the early stages of topic selection. Instead, think of presenting ideas in writing to a professor as a way to begin a concrete, specific dialogue with your audience.

✍ Guideline 2.4

Consider brainstorming a list of possible topics.

The basic premise of brainstorming is to produce (and usually tape-record or write down) ideas uncritically. Brainstorming usually works best when conducted by a small group, so you might want to form a group of fellow students for this activity. Group members generate ideas (often in response to ideas suggested by others in a back-and-forth oral dialogue) without criticizing each other's ideas. The reason for not criticizing them is that criticism can inhibit spontaneity and creativity.

At some later point, of course, you and/or your group will need to critically evaluate the ideas generated by a brainstorming session. Sometimes, you will find that combining ideas generated during brainstorming will produce a creative, useful topic for a literature review.

✍ Guideline 2.5

Consider starting by initially selecting broad topics and then narrowing them by adding delimitations.

A delimitation is a restriction on a topic. For instance, a broad topic such as "compliance with physicians' directions by patients" could be delimited in a number of ways. Examples 2.5.1 through 2.5.4 show some possibilities. Note that by adding delimitations, you are making your topic narrower. Avoid the temptation to add so many delimitations that your topic becomes too narrow.

Example 2.5.1
Sample topic delimited by age of patients:
Compliance with physicians' directions by elderly patients.

Example 2.5.2
Sample topic delimited by type of compliance:
Compliance with physicians' directions regarding medications.

Example 2.5.3
Sample topic delimited by type of disease:
Compliance with physicians' directions by patients with diabetes.

Example 2.5.4
Sample topic with two delimitations (type of compliance and type of disease):
Compliance with physicians' directions regarding medications by patients with diabetes.

A common way to delimit a topic is to restrict it by using one or more demographic variables. A demographic variable is a background variable with two or more categories. By selecting one or more of the categories and using them as delimitations, you can narrow your topic. The first column in Box 2B shows some demographic variables widely examined in research. The second column gives samples of categories that might be used when delimiting a topic.[1] The first demographic variable in the box is "age"; its use was illustrated in Example 2.5.1 above. The second one is "education, classification." You might, for example, delimit your topic to "gifted."

Of course, you can use more than one category to delimit a topic, as illustrated in Example 2.5.5, in which two categories of level of education (high school and college) are used.

Example 2.5.5
Sample topic with three delimitations (type of compliance, type of disease, and level of education [with two categories for level of education]):
Compliance with physicians' directions regarding medications by high school and college graduates with diabetes.

Note that you should have a rationale for the selection of delimiters. For instance, cognitive factors associated with medical compliance might be quite different for those with low levels of education than for those with more education, which would be a rationale for delimiting the topic in Example 2.5.5.

If you add too many delimitations (e.g., including only certain categories of age, gender, and socioeconomic status in addition to the three delimiters in Example 2.5.5) or select inappropriate delimiters (e.g., including certain hobbies and only certain political affiliations to the example), you may not find enough literature on your topic to meet the requirements for your literature review. Errors such as these will become obvious when you search the literature because you will find very little, if any, literature on topics with either too many or highly inappropriate delimiters. Techniques for searching for literature are covered in the next two chapters.

---

[1] Not all demographics are appropriate for all topics. An example: It would be inappropriate to use political affiliation as a delimiting variable in a literature review of the emotional status of people who have recently been diagnosed with breast cancer (e.g., it would be inappropriate to plan to review literature on the emotional status of only Republicans who have recently had the diagnosis). When a demographic is highly inappropriate to a topic, there will be little, if any, literature on the topic.

Box 2B *Sample demographic variables and categories.*

Sample demographic variables for delimiting topics:	Sample categories that might be used to delimit topics:
age	elderly
education, classification	gifted
education, highest level of	college graduate
education, type of	vocational
employment, length of	newly hired
employment status	employed part-time
ethnicity/race	Caucasian
extracurricular activities	competitive sports
gender	male
group membership	union member
health, mental disorder	depressed
health, overall status	poor health
health, physical disease	diabetes
hobbies	gardening
household composition	intact family with children
income, household	$20,000 to $35,000
income, personal	high income
language preference	Spanish
marital status	divorced
nationality, current	Canadian
national origin	Mexico
occupation	nurse
place of birth	Korea
political activism	votes regularly
political affiliation	independent
relationship status	divorced
religion, affiliation	Greek Orthodox
religiosity	attends religious services often
residence, place of	New York City metropolitan area
residence, type of	homeless
sexual orientation	heterosexual
size of city/town/area	large urban area
socioeconomic status (SES)	middle SES

⮌ Guideline 2.6

Scan titles (and abstracts) of articles in your topic area early in the process of selecting a topic.

Scan journal articles and their abstracts (i.e., summaries of articles that are usually published near the beginning of articles) in your general area of interest. For example, if you are writing a literature review for a social psychology class, scan the titles of articles in journals such as the *Journal of Personality and Social Psychology*. While an introductory social psychology textbook covers broad, major issues, journal articles tend to deal with very specific issues. Scanning titles may help you identify a reasonably narrow issue on which to write a literature review.

Many of my students have been surprised at the wide variety of interesting topics covered in academic journals. The titles shown in Example 2.6.1 piqued my interest. (Of course, what is "interesting" is in the eye of the beholder.) Each provides ideas for possible literature review topics. For example, the first title suggests the possibility of examining the literature on various types of commitment in intimate relationships.

Example 2.6.1
Five "interesting" journal titles identified by a quick scan of recent issues of the Journal of Personality and Social Psychology:

1. Approach versus Avoidance: Different Types of Commitment in Intimate Relationships[2]

2. Coping in Context: Sociocultural Determinants of Responses to Sexual Harassment[3]

3. Does Self-Love Lead to Love for Others?: A Story of Narcissistic Game Playing[4]

4. Why Do We Punish?: Deterrence and Just Deserts as Motives for Punishment[5]

5. Victim and Offender Accounts of Interpersonal Conflict: Autobiographical Narratives of Forgiveness and Unforgiveness[6]

---

[2] Frank & Brandstaetter (2002, p. 208).
[3] Wasti & Cortina (2002, p. 394).
[4] Campbell, Foster, & Finkel (2002, p. 340).
[5] Carlsmith, Darley, & Robinson (2002, p. 284).
[6] Zechmeister & Romero (2002, p. 675).

Note that all the articles for which the titles are given in Example 2.6.1 contain numerous references to related literature that you might use in refining your topic or cite in your literature review. For instance, the article with the first title in Example 2.6.1 (on types of intimate relationships) has many references, including the ones in Example 2.6.2. From the titles, these references seem to be "direct hits" for the topic at hand. Each of them will undoubtedly contain additional references to literature on the topic.

Example 2.6.2

Three closely related articles on intimate relationships identified by examining the references in the first article in Example 2.6.1:

1. Level of Commitment, Mutuality of Commitment, and Couple Well-Being[7]

2. Willingness to Sacrifice in Close Relationships[8]

3. Toward a Theory of Commitment[9]

It is also worth noting that the author of the first article in Example 2.6.1 also cited a number of articles with titles that clearly indicate the topic as *organizational commitment* (as opposed to *intimate commitment*) such as: "Organizational Commitment, Turnover, and Absenteeism: An Examination of Direct and Interaction Effects."[10] Such related topics might influence your topic selection. For instance, while you might have a strong personal interest in interpersonal commitment, you might have career goals such as working in business administration, which might make a literature review on organizational commitment more appropriate in terms of your long-term professional goals.

Note that the last title in Example 2.6.2 contains the word "theory," which leads us to the next guideline.

---

[7] Drigotas, Rusbult, & Verette (1999, p. 389).
[8] Van Lange, Rusbult, Drigotas, Arriaga, Witcher, & Cox (1997, p. 1373).
[9] Lydon (1996, p. 191).
[10] Somers (1995, p. 49).

ꕥ Guideline 2.7

Consider selecting a topic on which there is theoretical literature.

Theories help advance science by providing principles that explain the dynamics of a variety of findings. For instance, one published review of literature examined 70 empirical studies on perceived organizational support (POS) theory.[11] In brief, the theory suggests that "…employees develop *global beliefs* concerning the extent to which [an] organization values their contributions and cares about their well-being." (p. 698) [Emphasis added.] Also, according to POS theory, employees tend to assign humanlike characteristics to the organizations that employ them (i.e., the characteristics personify the organizations). Finally, note the word "perceived" in the name of the theory. According to the theory, employees' *perceptions* of organizations' commitment to them are the key—*not* the perceptions of management or others such as employees of governmental agencies that regulate businesses. As the authors of the review article point out, POS theory leads to a number of predictions about the behavior of employees, some of which are shown in Example 2.7.1.

> **Example 2.7.1**
>
> *A sample of important predictions from perceived organizational support (POS) theory*:
>
> Employees who perceive strong organizational support within a given organization (in contrast with those who perceive weak organizational support) should:
>
> 1. report greater job satisfaction,
> 2. have stronger feelings of competence and worth,
> 3. be more productive in their standard job activities,
> 4. take actions (beyond their standard ones) that help the organization, and
> 5. have fewer incidences of tardiness and absenteeism.

To the extent that theories are true, they often can help in practical problem solving. For instance, many employers try to reduce tardiness by

---

[11] Rhoades & Eisenberger (2002, pp. 698–714).

imposing penalties. (See point 5 immediately above.) However, creating an atmosphere in which employees perceive that the personified organization is committed to them might not only help reduce tardiness but might also have other beneficial effects such as taking actions beyond the standard ones to help the organization. (See point 4 immediately above.) Put another way, theories often provide solutions that have multiple benefits because each accounts for a number of variables.

Because theories help to unify our thinking about problem areas, often lead to important predictions, and often help in practical problem solving, consider whether there is theoretical literature on the topics you are considering for review. Other things being equal, select a topic with one or more theoretical bases instead of a topic that has not been tied to theory.

⭒ Guideline 2.8
Consider selecting a theory as the topic for a literature review.

The previous guideline suggests that you consider selecting a topic (such as types of intimate relationships) on which there is theoretical literature. In contrast, this guideline suggests that you review the literature on a theory, regardless of the topics to which the theory is applied. Textbooks in content areas usually describe major theories, which you might consider as topics. Less well-known and emerging theories, which might be of more interest to you, can be identified through a literature search, which we will consider in the next chapter. At this point, however, note that the term "theory" can be used in searches of databases in which literature is abstracted.

Because the consideration of theories is important in this chapter as well as in later ones, consider the formal definition of the term "theory" that is shown in Box 2C. As you know, a *set* is a group or collection of items. A set is *coherent* when its items are both related to each other logically and are consistent with each other.

Box 2C *Definition of "theory."*

> "A *theory* is a *coherent set* of hypothetical, conceptual, and pragmatic principles forming the general frame of reference for a field of inquiry (as for deducing principles, formulating hypotheses for testing, undertaking actions)." [Emphasis added.][12]

It is important to note that writers sometimes use the term *models* interchangeably with the term *theory*. Strictly speaking, the term *model* should be reserved for reference to how a *particular* set of operations works and interacts. For example, one might develop a model of how faculty on college/university campuses communicate by studying the particular lines of communication that are typical on campuses and the types of content typically communicated on campuses. In contrast, a *theory* typically is less restrictive and has the potential for use in many situations. For instance, social exchange theory is a communication theory that indicates that people assess communications in terms of payoffs (the "what's in it for me?" approach). It also suggests that the accuracy of the assessment of payoffs is dependent on the accuracy of the content that is being exchanged. As you can see, such a *theory* is not specific to communication in a particular setting or for a particular group. Instead, it can be applied to a wide variety of communication situations such as communications among religious groups, large corporations, neighborhood associations, and so on.

In terms of selecting a topic, a corollary to the guideline we are considering is that you may want to consider reviewing the literature on a model (such as models of communication processes on campuses) *or* on a theory (such as social exchange theory).[13]

⌗ Guideline 2.9

Consider preliminary definitions of the terms in the topics you are considering.

---

[12] Merriam-Webster Unabridged Dictionary accessed at http://unabridged.merriam-webster.com/cgi-bin/unabridged?va=coherent on August 28, 2002.

[13] For more information on social exchange theory, see Griffin (1994).

Suppose you are considering "power sharing among couples" as a possible topic on which to write a literature review. You will, of course, need to define both "power sharing" and "couples." For example, your definition of power sharing could include financial power sharing, child-rearing power sharing, recreational power sharing, and so on. If you find little literature on one type of power sharing, you might want to use a broad definition and include several types. If you find much, you might want to restrict it to just one or two types of power sharing. We will consider searching the literature in the next chapter.

Looking up topic terms in a standard dictionary is often useful. Consider the innocent-sounding word "couples" in the previous paragraph. Example 2.9.1 shows just a small part of the definition of the term "couple" (when used as a noun) in an unabridged dictionary. Compare definitions **a** and **d** in the example. Would you be interested in reviewing literature on power sharing among married couples *or* power sharing among unmarried couples who work together cooperatively in their occupations?

Example 2.9.1
Dictionary definition of a seemingly simple-to-define term ("couple"):

1. a : a man and his wife : a man and woman married or engaged <she and John would make a lovely *couple*—John Galsworthy> **b** : a man and woman paired as partners in any work, recreation, or other activity **c** : a man and wife employed together to perform usually related jobs in a single establishment (as butler and cook in a household) **d** : any two persons paired together in some work, enterprise, or activity[14]

✢ Guideline 2.10

If your literature review will introduce your original empirical research, strive for a close fit between the topic(s) reviewed and the variables studied in your research.

---

[14] Merriam-Webster Unabridged Dictionary accessed at http://unabridged.merriam-webster.com/cgi-bin/unabridged on September 5, 2002. (Note: Access to the unabridged version requires a subscription.)

Most reports of original research begin with an introduction that includes a literature review.[15] Unless your audience (such as your professor) indicates otherwise, the topic reviewed should closely match the variables studied. For instance, if you will be conducting a study on a specific technique for teaching reading using phonics, it usually would be inappropriate to select a topic as broad as "teaching reading" for your literature review. In fact, there is so much literature just on phonics, you would probably want to delimit your topic to some aspect of the use of phonics in teaching reading. By delimiting it, your literature review will help to introduce the report of your specific empirical study without diverting your readers with a discussion of literature on extraneous issues.

✍ Guideline 2.11
Consider your orientation and whether a topic you are considering lends itself more to qualitative or quantitative analysis.

Many issues naturally lend themselves to quantitative studies. For example, suppose you want to review the literature on the unemployment rate in rural areas of the United States. Because unemployment rates are statistical, your review might, of necessity, cover much quantitative material. In addition to economics, other examples of areas in which studies tend to be quantitative are many areas of geography (such as demographic studies), many areas of health (such as survival rates and the outcomes of prescription drug trials), and many areas of criminology (such as statistical studies of prison populations). If you are not quantitatively oriented, you might want to avoid these types of topics to the extent permitted by your audience's needs and expectations.

New areas of investigation often are examined with qualitative studies. Many others are examined in both quantitative and qualitative studies.

---

[15] For a thesis or dissertation, you may be required to write a chapter that introduces the topic and a separate chapter that reviews the literature. For journal articles, the introduction and literature review are typically integrated with each other.

Determining the orientation of the majority of the research on a topic will be discussed in the next chapter.

⚘ Guideline 2.12
Consider reviewing the literature on instrument(s) or assessment procedure(s).

When empirical research (i.e., research in which original research is conducted through observation of some type) is conducted, researchers use instruments such as tests, personality scales, questionnaires, and interview schedules. Almost without exception, instruments in the social and behavioral sciences have many limitations. The most important considerations in evaluating instruments are validity and reliability, which, arguably, are not perfect for any instrument. (These considerations will be discussed in Chapter 7.)

Suppose, for example, you are interested in the construct called "anxiety." You might review the literature on the Beck Anxiety Inventory (BAI), which has been widely used to study anxiety in a variety of populations and situational contexts. Your review might cover the history of attempts to measure anxiety (and its historical as well as current definitions), followed by a description of the development of the BAI, which was designed to measure anxiety as a trait separate from depression (an important issue because the two variables tend to vary together), and in what types of studies the BAI has been used in recent research. Those who read your review will obtain an understanding of the nature of anxiety (as we currently understand it, at least from the point of view used to develop the BAI) and the limitations of research on anxiety in general (because the quality of the published research is limited by the quality of the instruments used to measure it).

⚘ Guideline 2.13
Select a topic with an eye toward your future goals and activities.

This guideline was alluded to near the end of the discussion of Guideline 2.6. However, it is important enough to deserve to be stated as its own guideline. The most common future goals and activities are your career aspirations and your future academic pursuits. Note that when applying for admission to an advanced degree program, you may be asked to provide a sample of your writing. If your literature review is on a topic related to the program, it might be an excellent paper to submit as a writing sample.

Exercise for Chapter 2

1. Write very brief descriptions of at least two preliminary topic ideas in which you have a personal interest.

2. Evaluate each idea you wrote down for question 1 on a scale from 5 (highly appropriate for the intended audience) to 1 (highly inappropriate).

3. If your audience is your professor (or committee of professors), how clear are his or her expectations at this point in time? Write down any questions about expectations that you want to ask at the next class meeting.

4. Have you examined any model literature reviews? If so, which ones or which types (e.g., the ones at the end of this book *or* sample reviews written by students in previous semesters *or* ones in other sources such as academic journals)? If yes, did examining them help you? Why? Why not?

5. Name a broad topic in which you are interested. Delimit it by using one category of one of the sample demographic variables in Box 2B in this chapter.

6. Further delimit the answer you wrote for question 5 by using one or more additional categories for one or more of the demographic variables in Box 2B.

7. Can you think of demographic variables that are not included in Box 2B but which might be important in your field? If so, name them.

8. Scan the titles of the articles in at least three issues of the same academic journal. Use a journal appropriate to your field of study. (Note that the contents of many journals can be accessed electronically even if the entire articles are not posted on the Web.) Are any of the titles of articles interesting to you? If yes, name them.

9. At this point, would you be interested in reviewing the literature on a theory (or model)? Explain. (See Guideline 2.8.)

10. At this point, would you be interested in reviewing the literature on a topic on which the research is probably highly quantitative? Explain. (See Guideline 2.11.)

11. At this point, would you be interested in reviewing the literature on instrument(s) or assessment procedure(s)? Explain. (See Guideline 2.12.)

12. Do you have any specific future goals and/or activities that might influence your selection of a topic? If so, describe them.

Chapter 3

Searching for Literature and Refining the Topic

The processes of searching for literature and refining your topic are intertwined because the amount of literature you find on a topic of interest to you will determine whether you need to broaden it (to find more literature) or narrow it (to retrieve less literature). In addition, as you sample the literature on a topic, you may discover related topics that are of even greater interest to you.

This chapter is based on the assumption that you will be conducting an electronic search for literature. Note that almost all databases designed to assist in the location of literature have been computerized and are available via the Internet.

Many of the examples of the results of literature searches in this chapter are from the PsycARTICLES database, which is published electronically by the American Psychological Association (APA).[1] At the time of this writing, it contains more than 25,000 searchable full-text articles from 42 journals published by APA and allied organizations. Psychology students will also want to examine PsycINFO, which contains abstracts (i.e., summaries) of more than 1.5 million references to both APA and non-APA journal articles and books. You should be able to access these databases using the resources of your college or university library. If you do not have access via your library, you can purchase a personal subscription. Visit www.apa.org for more information.

---

[1] Unless otherwise specified, PsycARTICLES searches for this chapter were conducted using "all fields" (as opposed to just the "title field," the "abstract field," or some other restrictive field).

Almost all academic fields have one or more major electronic databases that assist in the search for literature on a topic. In education, the major one is Educational Resources Information Center (ERIC), which at the time of this writing, contains references to more than 1 million records that provide citations for journal articles, books, conference papers, and so on. Some of the results in the examples in this chapter are from searches of the ERIC database.[2] An especially useful electronic feature of ERIC is the AskERIC's Question and Answer (Q & A) Service. You can e-mail a question, and within two business days, you will receive a personalized response (generated by a person who is a specialist in using the ERIC database)—*not* an automated, computer-generated form-letter response. At the time of this writing, AskERIC can be accessed on the Internet by going to www.askeric.org/Qa/.

ERIC defines "education" in its broadest sense (i.e., *not* as a field devoted only to classroom and curriculum issues). For instance, a sociology student interested in reviewing literature on the homeless could do a "simple search" in ERIC, which at the time of this writing, retrieved references to 1,585 documents on the homeless. Restricted to only journal articles, the search retrieved 591 journal articles. Likewise, a business student using the term "advertising" would find 5,795 documents by conducting a "simple search." Restricting the search to only journal articles, the search retrieved 1,613. As you can see by these examples, an ERIC search will probably be fruitful for students interested in any topic that deals with human behavior.

Box 3B shows the output for one of the articles on advertising. Note that on the first line, the ERIC_NO (i.e., ERIC number) is EJ638975. When the six-digit number begins with EJ, it is a journal article. (EJ stands for "educational journal"; however, note that ERIC searches a wide variety of journals—not just ones with "education" in their titles.) When the six-digit number begins with ED, it is an unpublished document such as a conference paper or government report. (ED stands for "educational document.") Go to www.eric.ed.gov/ to visit the home page of the entire ERIC system.

---

[2] Unless otherwise specified, all ERIC searches were restricted to journal articles using "key words." Visit ERIC on the Web to learn more about its key words system.

Box 3A *The value of AskERIC.*

> Free, personalized responses via the AskERIC Question and Answer Service (www.askeric.org/Qa/) on the Internet can be helpful for students in a wide variety of fields because ERIC defines "education" very broadly.

Box 3B *Sample ERIC entry for an article on advertising.*

> **ERIC_NO:** EJ638975
> **TITLE:** Looking for Meaning in All the Wrong Places: Why Negative *Advertising* Is a Suspect Category.
> **AUTHOR:** Richardson, Glenn W., Jr.
> **PUBLICATION_DATE:** 2001
> **JOURNAL_CITATION:** Journal of Communication; v51 n4 p775-800 Dec 2001
> **ABSTRACT:** Presents a critical review of academic work on negativity in political *advertising* that shows that the concept has been defined in ways that are too broad, insufficiently holistic, and too pejorative. Suggests exploratory data indicate that the component parts of negativity are: misleading claims, emotional appeals, one-sided attacks, and a "generally loathsome view of politicians." (SG)
> **MAJOR_DESCRIPTORS:** *Advertising*; Discourse Analysis; Negative Attitudes; Political Campaigns;
> **MINOR_DESCRIPTORS:** Communication Research; Higher Education;
> **IDENTIFIERS:** *Advertising* Effectiveness; *Political *Advertising*
> **PUBLICATION_TYPE:** *080*; 143
> **CLEARINGHOUSE_NO:** CS761932
> **ISSN:** ISSN-0021-9916
> **LANGUAGE:** English
> **ERIC_ISSUE:** CIJJUN2002

Note that access to the ERIC system is free. It can be accessed by visiting www.eric.ed.gov/, where you will find information about its services, history, and structure.

Other major databases include Sociological Abstracts (formerly SocioFile), Linguistics and Language Behavior Abstracts, Business Source Plus, Health Source Plus, MEDLINE/PubMed, Astronomy and Astrophysics Abstracts, and Social Work Abstracts. Academic libraries typically maintain subscriptions to the on-line versions of these databases (as well as to the APA indices and ERIC). These library subscriptions allow free access to the databases for faculty and students. Check for handouts in your library on its database subscriptions, and/or consult with a reference librarian to determine which databases are available. Also, note that there are highly specialized databases (not listed here) that you might be able to access through your library. You can identify these through library handouts and/or consultation with a reference librarian.

Box 3C *Identify the databases available in your library.*

> Check for library handouts that list literature databases that are free to students via the Internet, and/or consult with a reference librarian for assistance in locating appropriate databases.

✣ Guideline 3.1

Invest time in learning how to conduct advanced searches of a database.

Most databases will allow you to conduct very basic searches to locate literature relating to a term of interest to you. For instance, in ERIC this is called a "simple search"; in PsycARTICLES and PsycLIT it is called a "quick search." It is desirable to conduct a basic search to get a sense of the amount and types of literature available on your topic. However, before spending much time reviewing what you have retrieved from a basic search, read the introductory material for the database, which tells you how the database is structured, what its features are, and how to conduct an advanced search. If the database has a thesaurus of terms on which it is structured, review it for relevant terms to use in your search. These steps typically will make your search much more efficient and save you time in the long run. A number of the advanced search techniques that are available on major databases are described in some of the following guidelines. In addition, techniques that can improve your search of almost any electronic database are described in other guidelines.

Box 3D *Learn how to conduct an advanced search.*

> Taking the time to learn how a database is structured and how to conduct an advanced search will make your search for literature more efficient and will save time in the long run.

⚘ Guideline 3.2

Familiarize yourself with the Boolean operators: NOT, AND, and OR.

By using the Boolean logical operators, you can broaden or narrow a search.[3] For instance, consider the results of four searches shown in Example 3.2.1, which were conducted in the PsycARTICLES database. The example makes it clear that the operators NOT as well as AND *reduce* the number of references found, while OR *increases* the number.

Example 3.2.1

Number of journal articles identified using NOT, AND, and OR:

Term entered in database restricted to the years 1995 to the time this was written:	Number of journal articles identified:
depression	1,062
depression NOT treatment	816
depression AND treatment	246
depression OR treatment	2,654

Notice that when we add the number for "depression NOT treatment" to the number for "depression AND treatment," we get the total number for the term "depression" (816 + 246 = 1,062). In other words, by using NOT and AND, we have partitioned the 1,062 articles on depression into two distinct groups: those that include "treatment" and those that do not.

Suppose you want to write a literature review on the treatment of depression. For most purposes and audiences, a review that referred to 246

---

[3] The term "Boolean" is based on the name of the British mathematician, George Boole, who developed Boolean logic.

articles would be excessive. Some of the following guidelines will illustrate techniques for making a search narrower.

♆ Guideline 3.3
Consider using demographics to delimit your search.

Box 2B in Chapter 2 lists a number of widely used demographics. Staying with the same topic (treatment of depression) and adding the demographic "elderly" (i.e., treatment AND depression AND elderly), the PsycARTICLES database yields only 12 documents, which might not be sufficient for some purposes. Searching the information on how to use the PsycARTICLES database (which should have been done earlier by following Guideline 3.1), we find that the database uses the specific terms shown in Example 3.3.1 to refer to various age groups.

Example 3.3.1
Terms used by PsycARTICLES to refer to age groups:

Childhood (birth to 12 yrs)	Adulthood (18 yrs & older)
Neonatal (birth to 1 mo)	Young Adulthood (18 to 29 yrs)
Infancy (2 to 23 mo)	Thirties (30 to 39 yrs)
Preschool Age (2 to 5 yrs)	Middle Age (40 to 64 yrs)
School Age (6 to 12 yrs)	Aged (65 yrs & older)
Adolescence (13 to 17 yrs)	Very Old (85 yrs & older)

Conducting the search again using treatment AND depression AND *aged* (the term used by PsycARTICLES instead of *elderly*), the database yields 60 articles. Assuming that some of them will not be useful for one reason or another and that some will overlap with each other and can be referred to jointly, 60 references is a good number to start with for most literature review purposes.[4]

---

[4] Often, some references are not useful because their content is not on-target. For instance, an article on depression among the aged who are prison inmates might be beyond the scope of the review you are planning to write. Other references may not be useful because they are so fundamentally weak that they do not contribute to our understanding of your topic. Evaluating articles to determine their strengths and weaknesses is covered in Chapters 6 and 7 of this book.

Note that most databases have guides to the terms they use (often called a thesaurus of terms). You should refer to these in order to identify terms to use to make your searches of the literature more efficient and comprehensive. For instance, ERIC publishes the *Thesaurus of ERIC Descriptors*, which shows the terms the ERIC system uses. An important feature of the *Thesaurus* is that for a given term that you look up, there are suggested broader terms (identified as "BT") and narrower terms (identified as "NT") that will help you widen or narrow your search as needed.

↳ Guideline 3.4
Consider searching for theoretical literature on your topic.

In the previous chapter, we explored the desirability of selecting a topic on which there is theory. Adding "theory" to the search (i.e., treatment AND depression AND aged AND theory), yields only two articles. At first, this may seem to be a disappointingly small number. However, you have the 60 articles identified in the discussion under the previous guideline *plus* two articles on theory, which in this case, are "cognitive theory of personality disorders" and "developmental therapy theory." These will help you in preparing a discussion of theories in your literature review on the treatment of depression among the aged.

↳ Guideline 3.5
Examine the references cited in the literature that you locate.

Under the discussion of the previous guideline, only two theoretical articles were located. However, each article has a fairly lengthy discussion of the theories in question, which would provide you with an overview of each theory as it applies to the specific topic. Perhaps more important is the fact that each has numerous references to other literature, including a book on each of the theories, which are shown in Example 3.5.1. Even though the titles do not suggest that they deal with the aged, they are clearly on-target in terms of the two theories, providing you with sources that are probably more comprehensive than journal articles for obtaining information for creating theoretical perspective(s) in your literature review.

Example 3.5.1

Two books on theory identified in the references of the two articles discussed under the previous guideline:

Clark, D. A., Beck, A. T., & Alford, B. A. (1999). *Scientific foundations of cognitive theory and therapy of depression.* New York: Wiley.

Ivey, A. E. (1986). *Developmental therapy: Theory into practice.* San Francisco: Jossey-Bass.

⤴ Guideline 3.6

Search for the names of prominent individuals who have written on your topic.

Suppose your tentative topic is "teaching mathematics." An ERIC search using "teaching AND mathematics" yields 7,865 journal articles, which is obviously quite overwhelming. If you decide to add Piaget's name (a famous developmental theorist) to the search (i.e., "teaching AND mathematics AND Piaget"), we obtain a manageable 30 journal articles.

Note that the ERIC database also contains unpublished documents. In this example, the search was limited to journal articles (i.e., articles published in academic journals). Journal articles generally are of higher quality since ERIC does not judge unpublished documents on their merits (other than whether they relate to education). This argument is advanced by the fact that all journals have editors who select the best of the submissions for publication; they often do this with the help of peer reviewers and an editorial board.

Box 3E *Distinguishing between published and unpublished literature.*

Published journal articles tend to be of higher quality than unpublished documents (such as ERIC documents) because the review process for selecting articles for publication in journals is more stringent.

↳ Guideline 3.7
Consider using "history" as a term in your search.

Suppose one topic you are considering is "the effects of television on children." Using "children AND television AND history" in an ERIC search, you would find 30 journal articles such as the one in Example 3.7.1, which contains information on an important aspect of the history of the topic. This reference and the other 29 would provide material for presenting an historical context (if you so desire) in your literature review.

Example 3.7.1

A reference on children and television found by using "AND history" in an ERIC search:

EJ445162. Kunkel, Dale. Crafting Media Policy: The Genesis and Implications of the Children's Television Act of 1990. *American Behavioral Scientist*; v35 n2 p181-202 Nov-Dec 1991.[5]

↳ Guideline 3.8
Consider using "definition" as a term in your search.

In Chapter 2, Guideline 2.9 suggests that you consider how you will define the terms in the topics you are considering. This raises the possibility that using the word "definition" as a search term might be helpful. Even if doing this does not produce a large number of references, sometimes an especially useful reference that discusses definitions will be retrieved. For instance, a PsycARTICLES search using "panic attacks" AND "definition" retrieved the reference shown in Example 3.8.1. This could be a keystone article for a reviewer since it is a relatively long article that spells out definitions *and* their implications for research, which could be useful when reviewing research literature on panic attacks.

Although the word "definition" appears in the article's title in Example 3.8.1, it is also likely to appear in the abstract if definitions are emphasized in the article.

---

[5] Note that this reference is shown as it appears in the database. It was not formatted to conform to any particular style manual.

Example 3.8.1

The reference retrieved using "panic attack AND definition":

Definitions of panic attacks and panic disorder in the DSM-IV: Implications for research. By Barlow, David H.; Brown, Timothy A.; Craske, Michelle G. *Journal of Abnormal Psychology*. 1994 Aug Vol 103(3) 553–564[6]

♆ Guideline 3.9
Consider using an exact phrase match.

Using an exact phrase match will identify only literature that has the exact words of a phrase in the exact same order. Many databases allow you to do this by putting the phrase in either double or single quotation marks. In PsycARTICLES, using the phrase *school achievement* retrieved 653 journal articles. Using the phrase 'school achievement' (with single quotation marks for an exact phrase match) retrieved only those 26 journal articles that contained the exact phrase "school achievement."

♆ Guideline 3.10
Consider using truncated terms or wildcards to locate literature that is classified under a derivative term.

Suppose you wanted to review literature on a topic with reference to people whose national origin is Mexico. Searching PsycARTICLES using the term "Mexico" yields 107 journal articles. Searching using "Mexican" yields 68 articles. If we truncate the term by using an asterisk, which is the symbol for truncation in PsycARTICLES (i.e., using Mexic*), we retrieve 168 articles.

The advantage of truncation is that you get literature on all articles that contain a term starting with "Mexic" while eliminating duplicates. In other words, there are 107 with the word "Mexican" and 68 with the word "Mexico," which gives us a total of 175 articles (107 + 68 = 175). However,

---

[6] Note that this reference is shown as it appears in the database. It was not formatted to conform to the specifications of any particular style manual.

we know that some of these contain both "Mexican" and "Mexico" because the search conducted with the truncated term "Mexic" retrieved only 168. By conducting two separate searches instead of one truncated search, your two lists will overlap with duplicates, which is obviously undesirable since you will have to manually locate and remove duplicates from your list.

A wildcard allows you to leave out a letter or string of letters when you search. In ERIC, a question mark is a wildcard for a single letter. Entering "poet?" as a search term yields articles with words such as poet and poets.

⍭ Guideline 3.11
When you want to narrow your search to the most relevant literature, consider restricting your search to the title and/or abstract.

Suppose your topic includes the word "discipline." A search of PsycARTICLES yields 301 articles that contain the word in one or more fields. If, at its core, an article is focused on discipline, the word is very likely to be used in the title and/or abstract (i.e., summary). Searching for "discipline" in just the titles of articles retrieved 27 articles (a much more manageable number than the original 301). Searching for it in just the abstracts retrieved 280 articles, which is still quite large, but it probably weeded out some of the 301 that were less clearly focused on the topic of discipline. Requiring that the articles have the word "discipline" in *both* the title AND abstract is more stringent and retrieved only 21 articles.

⍭ Guideline 3.12
Consider using the word "review" in your search in order to find previous literature reviews on your topic.

If there are previous reviews on your topic, you can benefit greatly from them. First, you can learn from the reviews, critique and reinterpret them, as well as bring them up-to-date with new literature.[7] Authors of reviews often use the phrases "A Literature Review" or "A Review of the Research" in the titles of their articles. A search in ERIC using "cheating" AND "review" as search terms in journal titles retrieved the reference to the literature review shown in Example 3.12.1, in which the word "review" is in the subtitle of the article.

Example 3.12.1

The reference retrieved using "cheating AND review":

EJ567552. Whitley, Bernard E., Jr.. Factors Associated with Cheating Among College Students: A Review. *Research in Higher Education*; v39 n3 p235–74 Jun 1998.[8]

⅏ Guideline 3.13

Consider searching for the term "qualitative."

In the previous chapter, you were advised to consider whether the literature on the topics you are considering tends to be quantitatively or qualitatively oriented. Traditionally, if a research article is quantitatively oriented, its title and abstract will *not* indicate that fact. However, the fact that a study is qualitatively oriented is sometimes mentioned in the title and/or abstract of the article. For example, a "quick search" of the PsycARTICLES database for the word "qualitative" in the title of articles retrieved 38 articles, including the ones in Example 3.13.1, in which the word qualitative has been italicized. Searching for "qualitative" in the title OR the abstract retrieved 347 articles.[9] On the other hand, searching for the term "quantitative" in journal titles using the same database retrieved no articles, illustrating that quantitative literature is seldom identified as such in the titles.

---

[7] Of course, if you cite and critique a prior review, you are ethically bound to read the original sources that were cited in that review.

[8] Note that this reference is shown as it appears in the database. It was not formatted to conform to any particular style manual.

[9] Many other qualitatively oriented research articles do not contain the word qualitative in their titles or abstracts.

Example 3.13.1

Titles of three of the references retrieved by searching for the word "qualitative" in titles of journal articles (italics added for emphasis):

Psychological Parameters of Students' Social and Work Avoidance Goals: A *Qualitative* Investigation[10]

Quality of Life after Spinal Cord Injury: A *Qualitative* Study[11]

Voces Abriendo Caminos (Voices Foraging Paths): A *Qualitative* Study of the Career Development of Notable Latinas[12]

♧ Guideline 3.14
Consider searching a citation index.

Using some of the suggestions for searching literature described above, suppose you found a pivotal journal article written by Smith that was published several years ago. By using a citation index, you can identify other literature in which Smith's article has since been cited. This literature might provide alternative perspectives on Smith's article, some might critique it, others might report successful and unsuccessful attempts to replicate Smith's research, while still others might provide evidence for and against Smith's theory, and so on. Obviously, there is great potential for obtaining very valuable information by using a citation index.

When searching a citation index, do not be surprised to find that the author of the pivotal article (such as Brenda Smith) has cited herself in a number of other articles she had published since the time that she published the one you consider pivotal. This is not uncommon because a researcher (or theorist) will often pursue a given line of research (or theory development) over a period of years or even decades. You will want to read Smith's subsequent work because she may have obtained results in later studies that shed new light on the earlier findings that led her to a reinterpretation or expansion of (or even rejection of) the interpretation of the findings in the pivotal article that you had identified earlier.

---

[10] Dowson & McInerney (2001, p. 35).
[11] Duggan & Dijkers (2001, p. 3).
[12] Gomez, Fassinger, Prosser, Cooke, Mejia, & Luna (2001, p. 286).

Most academic libraries maintain subscriptions to the major citation indices such as the Social Science Citation Index, the Science Citation Index, and the Arts and Humanities Citation Index. These can be searched electronically if your library maintains an appropriate subscription.

⅏ Guideline 3.15

Maintain a written record of how you conducted your literature search.

Suppose you come to the conclusion that "few experimental studies have been published on the XYZ phenomenon." Such a statement might be challenged by a professor, committee of professors, or journal editors who are familiar with relevant experimental studies that you have failed to cite. By being able to state specifically which databases you searched *and* how you searched them, you can deflect criticism that you have been careless in your search. Also, by providing this information to them, they might be able to refer you to resources or suggest literature search techniques that might help you improve your search.[13]

It is important to make *written notes* of your search techniques from the very beginning of your literature search. It may be months (or perhaps even years in the case of a dissertation) before you are asked to describe the techniques you used. Relying on just your distant memory may cause you to give only an embarrassingly fuzzy answer to the question.

Concluding Comments

Although only two databases were used for the examples in this chapter, most databases have the same features plus additional ones not covered here. You will be able to conduct an efficient and comprehensive search of the literature only by studying the instructions and examples

---

[13] With the exception of reports on meta-analyses, which is covered in Chapter 11 of this book, authors of journal articles seldom describe their literature search techniques. Students who are writing theses or dissertations, however, might consider describing these either in their literature review chapter or in an appendix. Do this only after consulting with the chair of your thesis or dissertation committee.

provided on-line for each database you use. Pay special attention to any "advanced search" capabilities provided by a database.

As you examine the titles of the literature you have retrieved, you will see whether you need to take steps to limit your search (so that you will have a smaller number of references to deal with) or broaden your search (so that you will have a larger number of references). Trying various search techniques such as those described in this chapter will pay you back many times over by providing you with a highly suitable list of articles, books, and other documents on your topic.

Exercise for Chapter 3

1. Have you identified one or more databases that you plan to search for literature on your preliminary topic ideas? If so, name them.

2. Which of the following should retrieve more articles from an electronic database?

   A. discipline OR punishment
   B. discipline AND punishment
   C. discipline NOT punishment

3. Suppose for a moment that a topic you are considering is "career counseling." At the time of this writing, 2,038 journal articles were retrieved via a basic ERIC keyword search. Name a demographic variable that could be used to delimit the topic and, hence, retrieve a more manageable number of references.

4. At this point, do you know of any theories you want to cover in your literature review? Will you search for relevant theories when you search for literature? Explain.

5. Do you know the name of a prominent researcher and/or theorist who has published on a topic of interest to you? If so, name the topic, and name him or her.

6. According to this chapter, is adding the word "definition" in a search typically very fruitful? Is it recommended that you do this? Explain.

7. Will using an "exact phrase match" increase *or* decrease the amount of literature retrieved?

8. According to this chapter, under what circumstances should you restrict your database search to the title and abstract fields?

9. According to this chapter, should you abandon a topic if your literature search identifies a previously published review on the same topic? Explain.

10. Very briefly explain what a "citation index" does.

11. Has the material in this chapter convinced you of the need to make detailed written notes on how you search for literature on a topic? Explain.

12. Have you tried to use a database since reading this chapter? Did you examine the description of how to conduct an advanced search (if it is available)? Did you learn of any useful techniques not described in this chapter? If so, briefly describe them.

Chapter 4

Retrieving and Evaluating Information from the Web

When writing literature reviews, writers often need up-to-date information. Because of the ease of electronic publishing, the Web is more likely to have such information than conventionally printed materials. It is not uncommon for a journal article or book to be published a year after it was written.

Sometimes literature reviews begin with current statistics on how many people (and/or the percentage of people) have a certain characteristic or a particular problem. Suppose, for instance, that your general topic for a literature review is cigarette smoking by pregnant women. Examine Box 4A, which shows two possible first sentences for a review. The second one, which cites current statistics found on the Web, is stronger and more compelling than the other.[1]

Box 4A *The beginning of two possible first paragraphs for a literature review. The second one cites recent statistics found on the Web.*

---

1. Many pregnant women continue to smoke despite warnings from the medical community. This makes it important to review literature to identify effective programs that...

2. Approximately 17 percent of pregnant women smoked cigarettes within the last month, according to a recent national survey (NHSDA, 1999).[2] This makes it important to review literature to identify... effective programs that...

---

[1] Using simple, compelling statistics is appropriate in both qualitative and quantitative reviews.
[2] Retrieved at http://www.samhsa.gov/oas/2k2/PregAlcTob/PregAlcTob.htm on September 19, 2002.

Note that many sources on the Web post the latest available information, which may not be completely up-to-date. For instance, the information in Box 4A was the most current available (for 1999) when retrieved in 2002 for use in this book. Nevertheless, a journal article or book published in 1999 would probably contain even older statistics given the publication lag in conventional, hard-copy publishing.

Note that Web addresses (i.e., URLs) frequently change, Web sites often are discontinued, and access that might be free at the time of this writing might not be free by the time you try to access them. If you have difficulties locating Web sites given in this book, use a general search engine such as www.Google.com to locate newer sites, free sites, and so on.

✣ Guideline 4.1

FedStats is one of the most valuable sources of statistical information on the Web.

At www.FedStats.gov, you will be able to access statistics from more than 100 Federal agencies.[3] Prior to establishment of this Web site, writers needed to search for statistics agency-by-agency. While the FedStats site still allows you to do this, you can also search by *topic* and the FedStats search engine will automatically search all agencies for relevant links to federal statistics. This is important for two reasons: (1) you do not have to search each agency separately and (2) an agency that you are not aware of (or did not think of) may have statistics relevant to your topic.

For example, I conducted a topic search by first clicking on <u>Topic links – A to Z</u>, which produced a screen with the letters of the alphabet underlined. (As you know, Web links to other sites are usually underlined and/or are sometimes identifiable by other means such as the use of a different color for a link.) By clicking on the letter C, I obtained the extensive set of links shown in Box 4B. By clicking on the <u>Breast</u> link (the second link from the top), the links in Box 4C were obtained.

---

[3] Be sure to go to www.FedStats.*gov* and *not* www.FedStats.*com*. The latter is *not* a government site.

Box 4B *FedStats links for the letter C.*

Cancer:
-- *Atlas of Cancer Mortality in the United States*
-- Breast
-- Cervical
-- Lung
-- Mortality maps
-- Prostate
Charitable trusts
Children:
-- Administration for Children programs and services
-- Adoption
-- Aid to Families with Dependent Children
-- *America's Children* (ChildStats)
-- Behavior and social environment indicators
-- Child care
-- Child support enforcement
-- Cigarette smoking
-- Delinquency and victimization
    -- Delinquency case records
    -- Juvenile arrests
    -- Juveniles as offenders
    -- Juveniles as victims
    -- Juveniles in court
    -- Juveniles in detention and corrections
-- Drug use
-- Economic security indicators
-- Education indicators
-- Foster care
-- HeadStart
Health:
-- Child and infant
-- Indicators
-- Insurance
-- Population and family characteristics
-- Nutrition
-- WIC
Civil justice statistics
Coal
Commodity flow
Common cold
Communications:
-- Broadcast radio and television
-- Cable television providers by community served
-- Telephone industry and telephone usage
-- Wireless communications services
Computer and Internet use
Construction
Industry tax statistics:
-- Corporations
-- Exempt organizations' unrelated business
-- Partnerships
-- Sole proprietorship

Consumer Credit
Consumer product safety
Consumer Price Indexes
Consumption, energy
Corporations
Country profiles
Crime (See also *Law enforcement*):
-- Characteristics of crime
-- Children
-- Crime in schools
-- Crimes reported to the police
-- Criminal offenders
-- Drugs
-- Firearms
-- Hate
-- Homicide
-- Prison inmates
-- Terrorism
-- Victims
-- Violent
Criminal justice:
-- Corrections
    -- Capital punishment
    -- Inmates
    -- Jails
    -- Prisons
    -- Probation and parole statistics
-- Courts and sentencing
    -- Court organization
    -- Criminal case processing
    -- Pretrial release and detention
    -- Sentencing
-- Criminal record systems
-- Employment and expenditure
-- Federal justice statistics
-- Indigent defense statistics
-- Law enforcement
    -- Campus law enforcement
    -- Federal law enforcement
    -- State and local law enforcement
-- Prosecution
Crops:
-- Crop progress and weather, weekly
-- Data by county
-- Data by state, historic
-- Field
-- Fruits and nuts
-- Vegetables

Box 4C   *A large sample of the links obtained by clicking on* Breast*, which is the second link in Box 4B (under the main heading "Cancer").*

<table>
<tr><td>

Treatment
Information about treatment, including surgery, chemotherapy, radiation therapy, immunotherapy, and vaccine therapy
• Breast Cancer Treatment
[patients] [health professionals]
• Male Breast Cancer Treatment
[patients] [health professionals]
• Breast Cancer and Pregnancy
[patients] [health professionals]
• More Information

Prevention, Genetics, Causes
Information related to prevention, genetics, risk factors
• Breast Cancer Prevention
[patients] [health professionals]
• Genetics of Breast and Ovarian Cancer
• Postmenopausal Hormone Use
• Long Island Breast Cancer Study Project
• More Information

Screening and Testing
Information about methods of cancer detection including new imaging technologies, tumor markers, and biopsy procedures
• Breast Cancer Screening
[patients] [health professionals]
• NCI Statement on Mammography Screening
• HHS Affirms Value of Mammography
• More Information

</td><td>

Clinical Trials
Information on clinical trials and current news on trials and trial-related data
• Breast Cancer Updates
• Search for Clinical Trials

Cancer Literature
Resources available from the CANCERLIT® database
• Search CANCERLIT®
• CANCERLIT® Topic Searches: Breast Cancer
• CANCERLIT® Topic Searches: Cancer Genetics

Related Information
Other information, including reports about NCI priorities for cancer research and initiatives
• Breast Cancer Progress Review Group

Statistics
Information related to cancer incidence, mortality, and survival
• Probability of Breast Cancer in American Women
• Breast - U.S. Racial/Ethnic Cancer Patterns
• Data Sources

</td></tr>
</table>

♺ Guideline 4.2

State and local governments and their agencies (including state-supported universities) often post very current statistics on the Web.

While you can obtain information at the local level at FedStats, you can sometimes obtain more current statistical information from nonfederal governmental sources. This is true for two reasons: (1) the federal government collects data periodically, with years intervening in some cases, and (2) local agencies must report in a very timely manner to their superiors such as city councils and mayors. Example 4.2.1 shows the latest statistics on property crimes in Buffalo, New York, posted on FedStats at the time of this writing as well as the latest ones obtained by going directly to the City of Buffalo Web site.[4]

Example 4.2.1

Property-crime statistics for Buffalo, New York, from federal and local sources:

	FedStats Web Site	City of Buffalo Web Site
Year		
2001	not available	16,185
2000	not available	16,591
1999	17,436	17,436

↳ Guideline 4.3

Use the raw statistics from governmental agencies—not statistics filtered by politicians or others with special interests.

Government statistics are usually collected by civil service employees (not political appointees). While there may be errors in their work, there is no more reason to suspect them of deliberately biasing the data collection than to suspect any other type of researcher. However, some politicians may understandably be selective (and perhaps misleading) in choosing which statistics to report. Hence, it is usually best to obtain the original government reports either in print or via the Web rather than relying on second-hand reports of government statistics presented by politicians or special interest groups, businesses, or other organizations. However, as you will see in Guideline 4.5, those with vested interests in statistical information sometimes provide useful links or primary-source information (via the Web), which can be helpful when writing a literature review.

Note that in some cases, it is appropriate to present original government statistics in a literature review *and* discuss how they are interpreted by individuals and organizations with varying political points of view.

---

[4] Retrieved at www.city-buffalo.com/Files/1_2_1/Police/Crime%20Statistics.htm on September 19, 2002.

♺ Guideline 4.4

Consider consulting the Library of Congress' Virtual Reference Shelf on the Web.

The Library of Congress maintains a Web site titled the Virtual Reference Shelf. It is an excellent site for general references such as dictionaries, general history, abbreviations, genealogy, and so on. It can be found at www.loc.gov/rr/askalib/virtualref.html.[5] Box 4D shows the main links at that site. At the bottom of the home page (not shown in the box but clearly visible on the Web site) is a link for "Ask a Librarian," which can be a very useful service if you are struggling to find specialized information to use in your literature review.

Box 4D   *Links on the home page of the Library of Congress' Virtual Reference Shelf.*

Internet Public Library Reference Center
Librarian's Index to the Internet Refdesk

- Abbreviations
- Almanacs and Fast Facts
- Associations
- Awards/Prizes
- Books, Periodicals, and Publishing
- Business
- Calculators
- Clocks/Times
- Consumer Information
- Current Events On the Web
- Dictionaries/Thesauri
- Directories
- Domestic Arts

- Education
- Encyclopedias
- Genealogy, Biography, and Archaeology
- General History
- Health/Medical
- Language and Literature
- Law
- Libraries
- Maps/Driving Directions
- Political Science and Government
- Quotations
- Statistics
- Technology and Engineering (Weather)

Selected Subject Feature * Other Reference Sites * In the News

---

♺ Guideline 4.5

Consider accessing information posted on the Web by a variety of nongovernmental agencies, associations, and advocacy groups.

---

[5] Rather than typing (and risk mistyping) long URLs, it is sometimes faster to do a quick search on a major search engine such as www.Google.com using a term such as "Virtual Reference Shelf." Use the quotation marks around the terms (e.g., "Virtual Reference Shelf") to conduct an exact phrase match and exclude other Web sites that might have only one of the words such as "virtual."

A wide variety of associations post information (and statistics) on the Web. Following the link called "Associations" in the Virtual Reference Shelf (see Box 4D), you can identify hundreds of associations, many of which are quite specialized. For instance, there are employee associations such as the Southern California Association of Fingerprint Officers at www.scafo.org, which publishes an on-line journal titled *The Print* in which there are original articles as well as reprints of articles from other sources. In contrast, there are political lobbying and advocacy associations such as the Web site for the American Civil Liberties Union at www.aclu.org, which publishes a newsletter and sells inexpensive special reports such as *Unequal, Unfair, and Irreversible: The Death Penalty in Virginia*.

You should be more cautious when citing information found on Web sites maintained by advocacy groups. On the other hand, because of their special interest in certain topics, they may have more information than other sources. In addition, you might want to compare and contrast the points of view of opposing advocacy groups in your literature review.

You should also consider accessing information posted on the Web by corporations. Suppose you are writing a literature review on allergies for a health education class. Going to the home page for the drug Flonase® will provide you with a reference to an article in an academic journal.

Keep in mind that complete objectivity in research cannot be achieved, which we will explore in more detail in Chapter 7. All agencies sponsoring research (even nonprofit ones that have special tax status) have points of view that might influence what is researched, how questions are worded, how the sample is drawn, how the information is presented, and so on. Your job is to try to understand their points of view and identify information on the Web that is reliable and useful for the purposes of your literature review.

⅋ Guideline 4.6

Major search engines used by the public at large often provide helpful information for use in academic literature reviews.

At the time of this writing, www.Google.com is a popular search engine. Box 4E shows the main portion of the advanced search page. Assuming that I want to review literature on the "gender gap" in voting (but do not want to trace it back to the suffrage movement), I have entered "gender gap" for the *exact phrase*, entered "voting, vote, and voter" for *with at least one of the words*, and "suffrage" for *without the words*.

Box 4E *An advanced search for gender gap in voting without coverage of the issue of suffrage.*

Google™ Advanced Search

Advanced Search Tips | All About Google

Find results	with **all** of the words		10 results ▲▼ Google search
	with the **exact phrase**	gender gap	
	with **at least one** of the words	voting vote voter	
	without the words	suffrage	

Language	Return pages written in	any language ▲▼
File Format	Only ▲▼ return results of the file format	any format ▲▼
Date	Return web pages updated in the	anytime ▲▼
Occurrences	Return results where my terms occur	anywhere in the page ▲▼
Domain	Only ▲▼ return results from the site or domain	

e. g. google.com, .org   More info

SafeSearch   ◉ No filtering   ○ Filter using SafeSearch

This search retrieved an overwhelming 9,440 Web sites. By changing **Occurrences** (third line up from the bottom of Box 4E) from "anywhere in the page" to "only in the title," I obtained a list of only nine Web sites, which are probably worth a close look since the words were important enough to be in their titles. Scanning the URLs at the bottom of the listings, I noted that a number were posted by advocacy groups, several were posted by government agencies, and one was posted by a university. Example 4.6.1 shows the beginning of one, which discusses some statistical matters regarding the gender gap.[6] Note that the statistics in this example are secondary-source material, which you should confirm independently by referring to original sources. However, you should also note that the *interpretations* of the statistics are primary sources of information.

Example 4.6.1

An article on the Web retrieved by searching for "gender gap" in title:

NOW and the Voting Gender Gap

By Brian Carnell

Tuesday, December 12, 2000

The National Organization for Women keeps making a claim in its press releases about the recently concluded election that, while technically true, completely glosses over the reality of the election. Here's a random sample by Tanya Melich:

> Unlike Florida, the proof of our power is not sullied with statistical probabilities. Nationally, women gave Gore their vote by an 11 percent margin while Bush won men by 11 percent. In Florida, the margins mirror this national vote with women backing Gore and men Bush. Whether by age, education, or economic status, the pattern holds....

> This paragraph is disingenuous. Yes, the pattern holds by age, education, or economic status—unfortunately, it *does not* hold by race and by marital status. The so-called gender gap is in fact largely a racial gap. Black and Hispanic women broke overwhelmingly toward Gore, while depending on which polling data you rely on, Bush barely won or barely lost the white female vote. If, in fact,...

Example 4.6.1 reveals a problem frequently encountered when gathering information on the Web: The material that is referenced is undated. In this particular case, the quotation from Tanya Melich is from an undated Web source. Without dates, it is hard to follow the history or line of discussion on a topic. Note that some Web sites prominently display the date on which the site was last updated. This can be very helpful in determining whether you are reading current information.

---

[6] Retrieved from www.equityfeminism.com/articles/2000/000089.html on September 19, 2002.

☙ Guideline 4.7

Pay attention to the extension (gov, edu, org, com, and net) in the results of Web searches.

As you probably know, the extension "gov" in a URL stands for "government," "edu" stands for "education," "org" stands for "organization," "com" stands for "commercial," and "net" stands for "network."[7] These extensions can be helpful if you are sorting through a large listing of Web sites retrieved by a search engine. For instance, you might want to start with those with the extensions of "gov" and "edu" because they may be more likely to be nonpartisan and noncommercial.

As an illustration, I searched using the term "depression" on a major search engine. The sixth Web site in the list that was retrieved was titled NIMH-Depression. If I were not familiar with the acronym NIMH, I might have passed over it except for noticing "gov" in the URL for the site. Clicking on it, I opened a home page on depression maintained by the National Institute of Mental Health, a prestigious federal agency. This site contains a large number of fact sheets, summaries, booklets, and an important link that leads to other links to information on depression maintained on the Web by other organizations such as the Mayo Foundation for Medical Education and Research and the American Academy of Family Physicians. In general, highly reliable sources such as NIMH tend to link only to other reliable sources.

☙ Guideline 4.8

Consider clicking on "cached" when opening a Web site from a search engine.

Search engines often list the Web sites with their titles underlined or in a different color to indicate that they are links. However, when the option is available (such as in Google), it is usually more desirable to click on "cached" near the end of the description of the link than to click on the title

---

[7] Additional extensions are being issued, but these are the most common ones at the time of this writing.

of a Web site. By clicking on "cached," the words you used in your search will be highlighted in different colors from the other words, which makes it easier for you to locate your topic(s) within a Web site, especially if much material is presented on the site.

⚘ Guideline 4.9

When you find a Web site that is very useful, consider following the links, if any, that it provides.

While this guideline is alluded to in the discussion of Guideline 4.7, it is important enough to be stated as its own guideline. At commercial sites, the links provided typically lead to other commercial sites. However, at noncommercial sites, the links often lead to other noncommercial sources of information that are relevant to the topic(s) they cover. Highly reliable and/or prestigious Web sites tend to provide links only to similar Web sites.

Concluding Comments

In the previous chapter, we explored techniques for locating published literature—typically academic material published in hard copy form (and, sometimes, also published on the Web). In this chapter, we concentrated on using Web sources to obtain information directly—not just to identify hard-copy literature published somewhere else.

The mercurial nature of the Web is the source of both a major strength and a major weakness. The strength is that its quick "changeability" allows individuals and organizations to promptly post detailed, current information. Prior to development of the Web, the dissemination of information often had a publication lag of up to a year (or sometimes more) in traditional, hard-copy publishing. A major weakness of publishing on the Web is that almost anyone can post information (whether it is correct or not) without the scrutiny that the material would typically undergo if it were being published in hard copy. This is true because, unlike publishing on the Web, hard-copy publishing is expensive and risky to a publisher's financial status if too many of its publications are not successful in the marketplace. Hence, most traditional publishers take great care in the editorial process to check and cross-check the accuracy of content and the clarity of its presentation.

As the Web becomes an increasingly important source of information for those who review literature, it is important to establish criteria to consider when evaluating a Web-based source of information. In developing criteria, some of the considerations are:

1. Who sponsors the Web site in question? A government agency? A professional association? An advocacy group? A for-profit corporation?

2. Does the Web site present primary source material (i.e., original) or just secondary material, which typically should be avoided?

3. If secondary material provides the "factual" underpinnings of the content of a Web site, is the material analyzed thoughtfully and logically, hence, making an original contribution by presenting original interpretation(s)?

4. Does the Web site indicate when it was published on the Web and/or when it was last updated?

5. Are complete references to cited material given?

6. Does traditional, hard-copy literature that is more thorough and complete than the material published on a Web site exist? (For instance, does the Web site contain only summaries of more extensive hard-copy publications?)

7. Is the purpose of the site merely to persuade readers to take a position (such as a political position or a position that is favorable to a commercial product) rather than to provide information and well-rounded, logical interpretations? If the answer to this question is "yes," this does not necessarily mean that the site does not contain valuable information, but it does suggest that a reviewer would want to exercise considerable care and good judgment when using information from such a site.

Enjoy using the Web while searching for material to use in literature reviews. Explore it using search engines in various ways, and follow potentially interesting links. Taking time to explore thoroughly your topic on the Web may give you new perspectives and information that you might incorporate into your literature review topic, it may help you refine your topic, or it might even lead you to change to an entirely different topic that you find more interesting and/or important. These beneficial outcomes can result only when you allot sufficient time to explore the many strands of the Web.

Exercise for Chapter 4

1. Examine the two beginnings in Box 4A at the beginning of this chapter. Do you agree that the use of recent statistics from the Web makes the second one stronger than the first? Why? Why not?

2. Go to www.FedStats.gov and look up a topic on which you are considering writing a review. Make notes on how you conducted the search (e.g., by alphabetical topics, by clicking on a map, by searching press releases, and so on). Write down a few relevant statistics, if any, that you found.

3. Look up the Web site for the state or local government where you live. (You can usually find it by using a general search engine.) Explore the site. Does it contain any information on a topic that you are considering reviewing? Explain.

4. Google.com is mentioned throughout this chapter as a general search engine. Can you name others? (If not, search for others by going to www.Google.com and conducting a search for other search engines.) Do you have a favorite one? Explain.

5. In the discussion of Guideline 4.5, you read this statement: "Complete objectivity in research cannot be achieved." At this point, do you agree? Why? Why not?

6. As a general rule, what happens to the number of Web sites retrieved when you search for a term only in the titles instead of "anywhere on the Web pages"?

7. If you conducted a search on the Web and retrieved many more sites than you wanted, would you be tempted to skip over the ones with a "com" extension in their URLs? Why? Why not?

8. Seven questions that might assist in evaluating a Web-based source of information are provided in the Concluding Comments near the end of this chapter. Do you agree that all are important? Can you add any to the list? Explain.

Chapter 5

Taking Notes and Avoiding Unintentional Plagiarism

If you have selected a topic of interest to you, you will understandably want to start reading (or at least scanning) the literature as you collect it. It is important to start taking notes as soon as you start reading. Few things in academic writing are as frustrating as remembering an interesting fact, opinion, or other important material and being unable to relocate it because you failed to note it when first encountered.

In this chapter, the term "taking notes" is defined very broadly to include not only writing notes on paper (or cards), but also underlining or highlighting on a photocopy (or the original, if it belongs to you), using Post-It® flags, and making notes using a word processor.

Failure to take good notes from the very beginning can lead to a case of unintentional plagiarism such as the one described in Box 5A.

Box 5A *A case of unintentional plagiarism.*

> A student has read extensively on her topic and has given it considerable thought. As she begins to write, she recalls an especially interesting point of view she saw somewhere in the literature she collected and now wants to use it in her literature review. However, she did not make note of it and is having trouble locating its source. She believes that the point of view in question is quite logical, makes common sense, and, thus, is "obvious." Because of this, she decides that incorporating the point of view in her literature review without citing its source will not constitute plagiarism.

Failure to cite a source for an original idea constitutes plagiarism even if the idea (or point of view) is logical and makes common sense. Keep in mind that ideas that are *not* logical and do *not* make common sense would probably not be published in the first place. Even "obvious ideas" belong to the person who first uttered or wrote them. The citation decision chart in Box 5B should be helpful in determining whether or not to cite material.

Box 5B *Citation decision chart.*[1]

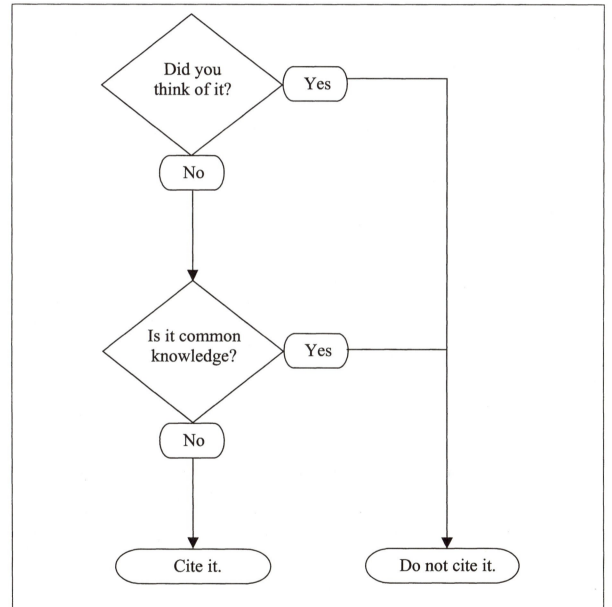

[1] From Harris (2001, p. 155). Copyright © 2001 by Pyrczak Publishing. All rights reserved. No duplication permitted without written permission from the publisher. Reprinted with permission.

ᛦ Guideline 5.1

Common knowledge does not need to be cited, but original expressions of it should be cited.

For instance, the meaning of the term *statistically significant difference* (i.e., a difference larger than would be expected on the basis of random error) is common knowledge among those trained in statistics. If you provide a routine definition in your own words, you do not need to cite a source. However, if you locate and use an original example that illustrates the meaning of the definition, you should cite its source. If you made a note of it while reading, you will be able to locate the source easily and cite it.

ᛦ Guideline 5.2

Even if you cite the ideas of others rephrased in your own words, the original source should be cited.

The definition of plagiarism in Box 5C makes this guideline clear. Italics have been added for emphasis.

Box 5C *A definition of plagiarism.*[2]

> "Plagiarism is the failure to distinguish the student's own words and ideas from those of a source the student has consulted. *Ideas derived from another, whether presented as exact words, a paraphrase, a summary, or quoted phrase, must always be appropriately referenced to the source*, whether the source is printed, electronic, or spoken. Whenever exact words are used, quotation marks or an indented block indicator of a quotation must be used, together with the proper citation in a style required by the professor [or other audience such as a journal editor]."

---

[2] From Harris (2001, p. 132). Copyright © 2001 by Pyrczak Publishing. All rights reserved. No duplication permitted without written permission from the publisher. Reprinted with permission.

⅏ Guideline 5.3

Failure to indicate clearly the beginning *and* end of summarized literature may lead to charges of plagiarism.

As you know, when you copy exact words, you should put quotation marks around short quotations and indent longer quotations, which clearly indicate where the quotation begins and ends. You also know that if you summarize literature written by others, you need to attribute it to them.

A special problem arises when another person's ideas are summarized in more than one paragraph, which is common in literature reviews—especially when discussing crucial pieces of literature. Compare Example 5.3.1 with Example 5.3.2. In both cases, all three paragraphs are summaries from a single source. Note that in Example 5.3.1, the second and third paragraphs might be taken to be original contributions of the person writing the literature review because there is no reference to the author (i.e., Wright). In contrast, Example 5.3.2 makes it clear that Wright's report is the source of the material in all three paragraphs.

Example 5.3.1

Three paragraphs that summarize a single source. (Unacceptable):

With the development of new telescopic methods, **Wright** (2002) was able to show that the coloration of the moon is....

Knowing the correct coloration of the moon helps scientists in three important ways....

Earlier studies failed to identify the correct coloration because of two serious flaws in their methodology. First, they....

Example 5.3.2

Three paragraphs that summarize a single source. (Acceptable):

With the development of new telescopic methods, **Wright** (2002) was able to show that the coloration of the moon is....

Wright also pointed out that knowing the correct coloration of the moon helps scientists in three important ways....

Earlier studies failed to identify the correct coloration because of two serious flaws in their methodology, according to **Wright**. First, they....

Notice that "Wright" is used three times in Example 5.3.2. In English composition courses, you may have been taught to avoid redundancy. However, in scientific writing, redundancy is not only acceptable but is desirable if it assists readers in understanding research reports and helps to identify clearly the sources of all ideas.

Keeping accurate notes on the sources of all ideas and clearly indicating the sources in your writing will help you avoid charges of plagiarism.

✑ Guideline 5.4
Establish criteria for the inclusion of literature in your review.

This guideline will help to keep your review focused on the key aspects of your topic. However, it is difficult to finalize selection criteria until you have started to read and make notes on the literature you have collected. This is true for three reasons. First, the body of literature that you have collected may have special characteristics that lead to the development of criteria that you could not anticipate in advance. Second, you may find that your criteria are so restrictive that very little literature can pass muster to be included in your review. Finally, your criteria may not be stringent enough, and you may find that you have an overwhelmingly large amount of literature to review.[3]

Consider the work of Akinbami, Cheng, and Kornfeld (2001). They established criteria for selecting literature on teen-tot programs[4] to discuss in their literature review. Some of the criteria are shown in Example 5.4.1. As a result of applying their criteria, the initial 46 published evaluations identified by the authors were reduced to just four. The authors provided a thorough review of these four evaluations. Of course, if your audience (such as your professor) requires more references, you might need to adjust your criteria so that they are less restrictive.

---

[3] As you know from earlier chapters, you can reduce the amount of literature to be reviewed by delimiting it to literature that deals with people who have only certain demographics. In this guideline, we are discussing criteria, such as methodological issues in research, that go beyond demographics.

[4] Teen-tot programs provide one-stop service centers to assist teenage parents and their children. A major goal is to help teenagers avoid additional pregnancies until they are financially and psychologically ready for them.

Example 5.4.1

A sample of the criteria for selection of literature on teen-tot programs:

1. Must describe a *comprehensive* program (e.g., clinical health supervision, assistance with staying in school…).

2. Must clearly describe the clinical component.

3. Must have statistical results—not just results described in narrative form.

☙ Guideline 5.5

Give each piece of literature a unique identifier such as the surname of the first author.

The identifiers could also be numbers such as 1, 2, and 3. Using identifiers can make your note taking more efficient and effective, which we will explore in the next guideline.

☙ Guideline 5.6

While taking notes, consider building a table that summarizes key points in the literature you are reviewing.

One way to organize your material initially is to build a table in which you list the identifiers (such as the surnames of the first authors) in the first column and special characteristics of each study in the other columns (with "descriptors" as headings.)[5] Example 5.6.1 shows a simple table of this type with descriptors such as number of participants, level of education, etc. Other descriptors could be added such as location of the study, methodology used (e.g., qualitative versus quantitative and/or experimental versus nonexperimental), socioeconomic status of the participants, and so on. Such a table will help you get an overview of the literature you are reading. If it is carefully constructed, you might want to include the table in your literature

---

[5] Tables are easy to build with modern word processing programs. For example, when using Microsoft® Word, click on "Table" at the top of the screen, then click on "Insert." From that point on, building a table will be obvious. If you want to use a large number of columns, switch from "portrait" to "landscape" (which will turn the page on its side so that it is wider than it is long) by clicking on "File," then "Page Setup," and then "Landscape," and then "OK."

review to provide your readers with an overview. In the narrative portion of your review, you will want to point out the highlights of such a table, but it is not necessary to repeat all the information in the table.

Because such tables provide only summary material regarding selected characteristics of the literature, your narrative should go beyond the contents of the table to discuss additional issues, relationships among various studies that are not obvious from the table, draw conclusions, and so on.

Example 5.6.1

A sample "notes table," which helps organize literature and provide an overview:

Identifier	Level of Education	Type of Measure	Number of Participants	Type of Assignment	Outcome
Applegate (2002)	College	Questionnaire	25 E, 20 C	Random	Sig. in favor of E
Brown (2001)	College	Interview	10 E, 10 C	Intact Groups (Nonrandom)	Diff. not sig.
Jones (2003)	General Adult Population	Observation	30 E only	(No control group)	Diff. not sig.
Chang (2002)	High School	Questionnaire	50 E, 50 C	Random	Sig. in favor of E
Solis (2003)	College	Questionnaire	110 E, 115 C	Random	Sig. in favor of E
Note. E = Experimental Group; C = Control Group; Diff. = difference; Sig. = statistically significant.					

An important advantage of a table like the one in Example 5.6.1 is that patterns you might otherwise overlook may become obvious. For instance, from the table it is clear that the three studies that had significant differences (all in favor of the experimental group) were conducted with random assignment, which is highly desirable in an experimental study. Note that experiments are almost always quantitative.

Tables can also be built for nonexperimental quantitative studies (such as surveys, which do not have control groups) as well as qualitative studies. Regardless of the types of studies you are summarizing in a table, it is recommended that the first column contain identifiers and that the remaining columns contain information on characteristics of participants, the types of measures used, and the outcomes of the studies.

Box 5D shows a summary table that was included in the published literature review by Akinbami, Cheng, and Kornfeld (2001), which was briefly discussed under Guideline 5.4. Because only four published evaluations were reviewed, it was possible for the authors to provide a considerable amount of information on each evaluation. If you are reviewing larger amounts of literature, consider including less information on each source to keep the table from becoming too large.

Box 5D *Sample summary table.*

Table 1
Teen-Tot Program Characteristics, Interventions, and Outcomes

Program	Intervention	Evaluated Outcomes	Strengths and Weaknesses
TEEN-TOT CLINIC. Nelson, Key, Fletcher, Kirkpatrick, & Feinstein (1982) • Duration: 18 mos postpartum. • Participants ($n = 35$): age < 17 yrs, race 91% black. Referred from urban hospitals. • Control group ($n = 70$): matched for maternal and child characteristics. Received care at public clinics.	1. Well-child health visits, developmental assessment, nutrition counseling, WIC, referral to community services.	1. 91% vs. 46% controls fully immunized (6 mos). * 97% vs. 83% controls between 5th–95th growth percentiles (6 mos).*	↑ Matched control group. No difference between participant and control group characteristics. ↓ No analysis of attrition. ↓ Many outcomes reported only at 6 mos. ↓ Small number of participants.
	2. Group sessions on child developmental and parenting skills.	2. [None reported]	
	3. Contraceptive counseling and services.	3. Contraceptive use (6 mos): 91% vs. 63% controls.* Repeat pregnancy (18 mos): 16% vs. 38% controls.*	
	4. Assistance with education, employment, living arrangements, goals, and relationships.	4. School enrollment (6 mos): 86% vs. 66% controls.*	
QUEENS HOSPITAL CENTER. Rabin, Seltzer, & Pollack (1991) • Duration: until mother 20 yrs old. • Participants ($n = 498$): age < 20 yrs, race not specified. Recruited from clinical adolescent program. • Control group ($n = 91$): from adult obstetric clinic. Received care in pediatric and adult family planning clinic.	1. 24-hour "on-call" system, each teen-infant pair assigned to one interdisciplinary team.	1. Clinic attendance: 75% vs. 18% of controls.* Maternal morbidity† and infant morbidity‡ lower among participants.*	↑ No difference between participant and control group characteristics. ↓ Length of participation not specified. ↓ No discussion of attribution or dropout characteristics. ↓ Intervals of outcome evaluation not specified.
	2. Family life education program with bi-weekly classes for participants, their partners and families.	2. Contraceptive use: 85% participants vs. 22% of controls.* Repeat pregnancy: 9% participants vs. 70% controls.*	
	3. Comprehensive services available on-site (mental health center, WIC, housing office, high school equivalency program, day care center).	3. School attendance: 77% participants vs. 38% controls.* School completion: 95% participants graduated from high school. Employment: 48% participants vs. 22% controls.*	**Continued →**

Box 5D *Continued*

Program	Intervention	Evaluated Outcomes	Strengths and Weaknesses
TEEN MOTHER AND CHILD PROGRAM. Elster, Lamb, Tavare, & Ralston (1987) • Duration: 2 yrs postpartum. • Participants (n = 125): age < 18 yrs, race > 80% white. 35% from high socioeconomic group. Self-referral, community referral. • Control group (n = 135): Recruited from WIC site. Received care from community providers.	1. Prenatal care, education, psychosocial and nutritional assessments. 2. Health care for infants and teen mothers. Staff on call. WIC referral. 3. Individual counseling about financial management, school, and work. Referrals for vocational training, education. 4. Contraceptive education. 5. Infant health and development education. 6. Counseling on parenting8, interpersonal relationships, and stress. Outreach to fathers.	1. Participants had more prenatal visits.* No difference in preterm or low birthweight. 2–6. Participants had better composite score at 12 and 26 mos postpartum* (repeat pregnancy, school/job attendance, receipt of entitlements, ER visits, hospitalizations, immunizations, maternal preventive health efforts, child developmental knowledge, and General Well-Being Schedule scores). Greater immunization completion among participants.* No significant difference in infant growth and development or repeat pregnancy rates.	↔ Participants more likely to have higher income, attend school, graduate, or be working at time of enrollment. Multiple regression used to control for differences. ↓ High attrition rate.
SPECIAL CARE PROGRAM. O'Sullivan & Jacobsen (1992) • Duration: 18 mos. • Participants (n = 120): age < 18 yrs, race 100% black. Recruited from urban teaching hospital. • Random assignment to control group (n = 123). Received routine care.	1. Well-baby visits. Participants received reminders if appointment missed. 2. Social worker reviewed family planning methods, made referrals to birth control clinic. 3. Health care provider asked about mother's plan to return to school. 4. Health teaching in the waiting room. Infant care and appropriate ER use education.	1. Clinic attendance (18 mos): 40% vs. 22% of controls. Immunizations (18 mos): 33% vs. 18% of controls.* 2. Repeat pregnancy (18 mos): 12% vs. 28% of controls.* 3. Return to school: > 50% of both participants and controls (no significant statistical difference). 4. ER use: 75% vs. 80% for controls (no significant statistical difference).	↑ Randomized study. ↑ Outcomes analyzed among dropouts. ↔ High attrition rate, but 91% of original participants and controls interviewed at 18 mos.

* Statistically significant difference using chi-square test (95% confidence level).
† Disease state of pelvic organs, upper respiratory, hematologic or gastrointestinal systems requiring multiple doctor visits or hospitalizations.
‡ Includes maternal morbidity definition plus any accident in a child under 2 years of age.
ER: emergency room
WIC: Women Infant Children program

♗ Guideline 5.7

Consider using color-coding while reading and making notes.

Color-coding while you are reading can help you quickly locate material as needed while you are writing your literature review. You might use one color for references to relevant theories, another for definitions of terms, another for results sections, and so on.

Color-coding can be done with pen highlighters and Post-It® flags on hard copies of literature or by using the highlighting, letter coloring, and note-making features of modern word processing programs if you have electronic copies of literature.

⮆ Guideline 5.8

Pay special attention to definitions while taking notes.

If different authors use different definitions of the variables you are reviewing, you will need to take that into account in your literature review. One possibility is to consider whether studies with one type of definition tend to have one type of result while those with another definition tend to have a different type.

Note that definitions sometimes change over time, making it difficult to identify trends in findings from earlier to later studies. For instance, "physical child abuse" tends to be more broadly defined today than it was by previous generations. Forms of physical punishment administered by parents and teachers that were considered acceptable at one time are now considered harsh and sometimes abusive. This change in definitions makes it difficult to make valid generalizations about whether such abuse has been increasing or decreasing across time periods.

As you know, the discussion under the previous guideline suggested that you use a special color to code definitions for easy reference when you begin to write your review. After color-coding definitions in a color such as green, you can quickly locate definitions to reread them and compare them with each other. If there are major differences among them, this fact should be discussed in your literature review.

⮆ Guideline 5.9

Pay special attention to researchers' descriptions of the limitations of their research methodology.

Authors of research articles often describe the limitations of their studies. While this may be done anywhere in the articles, they typically discuss them in the Discussion section near the end of their articles. Making notes on the limitations that are discussed (and perhaps color-coding them) may save you time when you consider the strengths and weaknesses of the various studies you are reviewing. Some researchers will provide extensive discussions of their study limitations, which you can then use to look for studies conducted by others who do not recognize or discuss their limitations. Example 5.9.1 shows some short excerpts from a lengthy statement of limitations that appears near the end of a research article.[6]

Example 5.9.1

Brief excerpts from researchers' self-critique mentioning limitations:

The study has three limitations. First, the investigation was conducted at a single site and we cannot generalize....

Second, the sample size limited the number of variables we could include in the analysis.... For example, client and clinician race or ethnicity...may play a role.... However, given the sample size, it would not have been statistically prudent to include a set of client and clinician characteristics....

Third, because the same individuals did the ratings [two sets of ratings]..., there could have been a response bias—that is, a rater's judgment on one scale could have influenced his or her judgment on the other scale. However....

↻ Guideline 5.10

It is misleading to read and make notes only on the abstracts of articles without disclosing the fact that you have done so in your review.

Most journal articles begin with abstracts that summarize the articles. Many journals put severe restrictions on the length of abstracts. (For example, the *Publication Manual of the American Psychological Association* suggests that they contain 120 words or less.[7]) Thus, researchers can cover only the most salient details in their abstracts, and reading only the abstracts and not the entire articles will provide you with only limited information on

---

[6] Loneck, Banks, Way, & Bonaparte (2002, p. 141).
[7] American Psychological Association (2001, p. 15).

the contents of the literature you have collected. Example 5.10.1 shows an abstract of typical length for research articles in the social and behavioral sciences.

Example 5.10.1

An abstract for a journal article of typical length:

This study examined the effects of a relapse prevention program (RP) and a 12-step continuing care program (for two years) on both depressed and nondepressed patients. Patients were randomly assigned to programs. Depressed patients attended more treatment sessions and had more cocaine-free urines during treatment than participants without depression, but they drank alcohol more frequently before treatment and during the 18-month posttreatment follow-up. Cocaine outcomes in depressed patients deteriorated to a greater degree after treatment than did cocaine outcomes in patients without depression, particularly in patients in RP who had a current depressive disorder at baseline. The best alcohol outcomes were obtained in nondepressed patients who received RP. The results suggest that extended continuing care treatment may be warranted for cocaine-dependent patients with co-occurring depressive disorders.[8]

Reading only the abstract in Example 5.10.1, a reviewer might make a note such as *Relapse prevention therapy is superior to 12-step focused group intervention (McKay et al. 2002)* and include the note in a literature review. Unless the reviewer starts the statement with a phrase such as *According to the abstract…*, readers will assume that the review was prepared with care and, of course, the entire article was read. Thus, reading and making notes on only abstracts without acknowledging that this was done is misleading and probably unethical. Most professors would prohibit such a practice.

Not reading the entire article and relying on only the abstract in Example 5.10.1 would leave the reviewer without knowledge of a vast array of important facts and issues that would have bearing on the evaluation of the research and how it should be treated in the literature review. Some of these are shown in Example 5.10.2.

---

[8] McKay et al. (2002, p. 225). For instructional purposes, this abstract was modified slightly.

Example 5.10.2

A sample of important facts and issues that would be missed if a reviewer relied on only the abstract shown in Example 5.10.1 instead of reading the entire article summarized by the abstract:

1. All participants were male veterans who were referred to the continuing care program at Philadelphia Veterans Affairs Medical Center. [Note: This is a highly specialized group.]

2. Most of the participants had already participated in a four-week intensive outpatient program at the medical center. [Note: This prior treatment may have interacted with the treatments in this study.]

3. Self-reports on cocaine use were validated with urine toxicology tests. [Note: The use of urine tests is an important strength of this study.]

4. The study had a very high follow-up rate. [Note: This is an important strength of the study.]

5. The study did not include biochemical tests to collaborate alcohol use. [Note: This is a weakness of the study.]

⚘ Guideline 5.11

Make notes on how other writers have organized the literature on your topic.

When you write your review, you will need to use some type of organizational scheme. For instance, you might start with how many people are affected by a problem, followed by a definition of a problem, followed by a discussion of relevant theories, and so on. Briefly examine Model Literature Review 3 on religion-accommodative counseling. It begins with some statistics on religious beliefs in the United States. Flipping through the pages of the review, you will see major headings that are centered in bold as well as second- and third-level headings that are in italics. These headings and subheadings indicate the organizational structure of the review.

There is no single organizational scheme that is suitable for all topics and audiences. As you read the literature on your topic, consider making notes on how others have organized their reviews on the topic. Note that even journal articles that present original empirical research on a topic often begin with brief literature reviews. It is a good idea to note how these are organized even if they do not have headings within the review.

As you begin reading and making notes, develop a tentative organizational scheme, and then modify it as you get ideas by reading additional literature. In the end, you should have an original scheme that is highly suitable for organizing the particular body of literature that you have reviewed.

Exercise for Chapter 5

1. Have you ever written a paper and had an ethical dilemma about citing a source for an idea (such as not being able to recall the source but wanting to use the idea anyway)? If yes, how did you resolve it?

2. According to this chapter, if an author presents original ideas that are logical and make common sense, should that author's work be cited?

3. State several facts, concepts, or ideas you believe are "common knowledge" whose sources do not need to be cited. Discuss them with your classmates to see if they agree with you.

4. Authors of a literature review wrote this statement: "Providing for defense and security is a singular and defining purpose of national government."[9] The context in which this sentence appears makes it clear that the authors are referring to the national government of the United States. The authors do not cite a reference for the sentence. Do you think that they should have cited a reference, *or* do you think the sentence makes a statement that is common knowledge? Explain.

5. Authors of a literature review wrote that approximately "5 of every 100 high school-age students drop out of school each year. This figure has

---

[9] Torres-Reyna & Shapiro (2002, p. 279).

remained constant for the past 10 years."[10] Do you think that the authors should have cited a reference, *or* do you think the sentence makes a statement that is common knowledge? Explain.

6. According to this chapter, does rephrasing the expression of the ideas of others relieve you of the responsibility to cite their sources?

7. According to this chapter, what might happen if you fail to indicate clearly the beginning *and* end of material that you summarize in a literature review?

8. Consider one of the topics on which you might write a literature review. At this point, can you think of any criteria that you might use for the inclusion (and/or exclusion) of literature? Explain. See Guideline 5.4.

9. At this point, do you plan to build a table to summarize key points while you take notes on the literature you collect? Why? Why not? See Guideline 5.6.

10. Name at least three characteristics that you might color-code when reading and making notes on the literature you collect. Name characteristics other than those mentioned in this chapter. See Guideline 5.7.

11. Briefly explain why it is important to pay special attention to definitions while taking notes.

12. According to this chapter, where do authors of research articles typically discuss the limitations of their studies?

13. Do you agree that it is misleading to read and make notes only on the abstracts of articles? Do you think it is unethical? Explain.

---

[10] Wood, Murdock, & Cronin (2002, p. 605).

14. Read the abstract for Model Literature Review 2 on predicting school violence. (Note that abstracts appear at the beginning of articles.) Then briefly scan the review for at least three important facts or ideas that would be missed by someone who read only the abstract. Write them here.

Chapter 6

Guidelines for Evaluating Sources of Literature

In this chapter, we will consider guidelines for evaluating *sources* of literature, with special attention to academic journals. In the next chapter, you will find guidelines for evaluating individual research reports, which most typically are published in academic journals.

✆ Guideline 6.1

Even the most prestigious sources sometimes publish seriously flawed material.

In every professional field, there are journals that are considered more prestigious than others. Often, those published by large professional associations or by universities are considered prestigious. If you are not sure which journals are considered highly prestigious in your field, talk with your instructor and other faculty members in your department.

Note that certain Web sites are considered more prestigious places than others to publish original research. At the current time, there are a number of Web-based journals in a wide variety of professional fields. Over time, some are likely to emerge as clearly more prestigious than others.[1]

The more prestigious journals typically receive many more submissions than they can publish. Hence, editors of these journals are able to select manuscripts for publication from a large pool of submissions. Nevertheless, there will be flaws in research reports in even the most prestigious journals because conducting research involves making compromises, leading to

---

[1] Many journals are printed in hard copy as well as on the Web. Some journals publish exclusively on the Web. Often, special subscriptions are required to access the online versions.

problematic choices in designing and executing a research study. This point is covered in detail in the next chapter.

Note that you should not judge a journal article solely on the basis of the prestige of the journal in which it is published. Box 6A shows some reasons why an editor of a highly respected journal (with the assistance of his or her reviewers) might decide to publish an article that has serious flaws in its research methodology.

Box 6A *Three reasons why methodologically weak articles are published.*

1. The topic of the article might be very *timely*. For instance, a methodologically weak manuscript on an infectious disease that is being covered widely in the mass media might be selected for publication in a medical journal over a methodologically stronger manuscript on a disease that is not of current general interest. This is especially true if there is little or no previously published research on the "timely disease" (or timely topics in fields other than medicine).

2. The article might have important *theoretical implications*. As you know from earlier material in this book, theory development is a major function of science because theories help us explain diverse observations and assist us in making predictions. An article that presents strong, logically constructed theoretical arguments (even if its research methodology is weak or questionable) has a better chance of publication than one that does not present such material.

3. The editors may be striving for *balance*. For instance, a journal devoted to family issues has published many articles on spousal abuse—almost all of which were on husbands abusing their wives. A methodologically modest research article on wives abusing their husbands might be published to provide balance and fill in a gap in the literature.

As a general rule, more prestigious journals (or Web sites) are more reliable sources of information than less prestigious ones. However, the strengths and weaknesses of an individual article published in any journal should be evaluated carefully by someone preparing a literature review. Guidelines for doing this are described in the next chapter.

⚘ Guideline 6.2

Consider who sponsors a publication. Professional associations, foundations, government agencies, and for-profit companies are major sponsors.

Professional associations publish journals, and sometimes publish books and pamphlets. Associations such as the American Association for Public Opinion Research, the Library Administration and Management Association, and the Society of Pediatric Nurses have large memberships. Consequently, they receive large numbers of submissions of manuscripts to be considered for publication in their journals. From these submissions, journal editors are able to select those that most closely meet their editorial policies and seem likely to make important contributions to the field.[2]

Foundations, government agencies, nonprofit agencies, and for-profit companies also publish journals and books in professional fields. Many of these have high standards and publish excellent material. It is possible that some journals published by for-profit companies are less selective than other sources in deciding what to publish.

⚘ Guideline 6.3

Check to see whether a journal (or publisher) has an independent editorial board.

---

[2] This does not mean, however, that they are free of flaws. Instead, it means that the content is appropriate for the journal and that the manuscript meets at least minimal standards for the expression of ideas, originality, methodological soundness, relationship to theory, and other criteria established by the journal's editors.

Editorial boards establish guidelines and policies for journals. Members of the boards also frequently serve as reviewers of manuscripts that are submitted (see the next guideline). The names of editorial board members are usually published near the beginning of each issue. Their independence is indicated by institutional affiliations that are listed with their names. Most editorial board members are affiliated with colleges and universities.

♨ Guideline 6.4

Check to see whether a journal uses a "blind" peer-review process when selecting manuscripts for publication. (This is also called a "juried process.")

Typically, the editor of a journal checks to see that a manuscript submitted for consideration for publication covers a topic within the field covered by the journal. If so, he or she submits it to several knowledgeable professionals (the jury of peers) for critical review. (Information regarding authorship is almost always removed, which makes the reviewers "blind" to the authorship.) The peer reviewers critique the manuscript (sometimes with a checklist) and make overall recommendations regarding whether it should be published. Often, they recommend that a manuscript be published contingent on the author making certain changes that the reviewers believe will improve the article.

Almost invariably, journals published by professional associations are peer-reviewed because the editors are accountable to the members of the associations. All members, and especially those whose manuscripts were rejected at some point in the past, want the process for selecting manuscripts for publication in their associations' journals to be done in a fair and objective manner.

It is not always easy to determine whether a journal is peer-reviewed. A major tip-off is if the "instructions to authors" states that all information indicating authorship or sponsorship should be submitted on a piece of paper that is separate from the manuscript. This usually indicates that there will be a "blind" peer-review (i.e., a review without the reviewer knowing the authorship).[3]

Approval through a peer-review process does not guarantee that the manuscripts selected for publication as articles will be strong from a research methodology point of view. (See Box 6A.) It does mean, however, that peers have judged them to contain information that will be useful to the professionals who read the journals.

Note that major publishers of textbooks also use a peer-review process in deciding which manuscripts to publish as books. Much of the material in textbooks, however, is considered "secondary" since it is often based on original works by others. When writing a literature review, aim to cite only primary sources whenever possible.

✎ Guideline 6.5
Consider the institutional affiliation of the author.

Articles in academic journals and books on academic topics understandably tend to be written by professors. Government employees and employees of private for-profit and nonprofit companies also write manuscripts for publication in journals. Sometimes, authorship will give you hints as to quality and objectivity. For instance, be cautious when the authors' affiliations (and perhaps the journals' sponsorships) are special interest groups that lobby for a particular point of view within the political system (e.g., gun control, abortion laws, and so on). While they may have solid data in which they firmly believe, you will want to evaluate such articles with extra care since the authors may have "blind spots."

Also, be on the lookout for authors (whether professors or not) who write research about products that they wish to sell or that their institutions sell (such as educational devices and testing devices). Their close affiliation with the products for sale does not in any way indicate that their research is fraudulent. However, it is helpful to have confirmatory research conducted by independent researchers on the effectiveness of such products. It is also

---

[3] Instructions to authors are usually published near the beginning of journals or at the end. Some journals publish their instructions in only one issue per year. Major publishers of journals maintain Web sites where these instructions can often be obtained.

helpful to know whether any widely accepted theoretical underpinnings were used in the development of the products.

☙ Guideline 6.6

Consider the overall quality of a journal in which an article is published.

By following Guidelines 6.1 though 6.5, you will have information that will help you judge the overall quality of a journal. Also, consider whether it seems to be professionally edited (e.g., free from mechanical flaws such as spelling and grammatical errors) and that there is overall consistency in quality from article to article. Journals that get only a small number of very good submissions and have to choose among poor ones to fill their journals tend to be second-tier journals.

Part of the "publish or perish syndrome" in academe is not only the question of whether a professor's research has been published but also whether he or she has been published in journals of high quality.[4] While this is a somewhat subjective matter, professors are aware that there are degrees of quality across journals and consider this when choosing journals to which they submit their manuscripts.

☙ Guideline 6.7

Journals that publish long articles are usually more important sources than those that publish short ones.

As you know, longer pieces of writing are not necessarily better than shorter ones. However, in many fields, there are journals that specialize in publishing large numbers of short articles—often no more than a few pages in length (on small-sized pages). While research articles in such journals may contain some useful facts that you might want to use in a literature

---

[4] Typically, recommendations regarding promotions and tenure for professors are made by committees of full professors who teach in the same or related fields. Because of their long participation in a field, they often know the reputations of various journals. Also, they often will consider whether a professor has published in peer-reviewed journals (see Guideline 6.4) as well as whether authors of other articles have cited the articles published by the professor being considered. The reference sections of libraries usually have citation indices that keep track of who is citing whom and in what publications.

review, the shortness of the articles precludes a thorough discussion of the rationale, methodology, findings, and theoretical underpinnings of the individual reports of research.

Exercise for Chapter 6

1. Very briefly name the three major reasons why methodologically weak articles are sometimes published (even in highly respected journals).

2. Name the major sponsors of journals (i.e., types of publishers).

3. What indicates the "independence" of an editorial review board?

4. Many journals use a "blind peer-review process" to assist in the selection of manuscripts for publication. What is the meaning of the word "blind" in this context?

5. In this chapter, a rationale is given for the statement that journals that specialize in publishing very short articles might be of lesser quality than those that specialize in publishing long articles. What is the rationale?

6. Does this chapter imply that you should cite in your review only articles published in prestigious journals? Explain.

Chapter 7

Evaluating and Interpreting Research Literature

In this chapter, we will consider basic guidelines for evaluating research literature. Although the emphasis is on the evaluation of research reports published in academic journals, the guidelines also apply to other sources of original research such as books, conference papers, speeches, and so on. All the guidelines apply to both qualitative and quantitative research reports. However, there are differences in how some of the guidelines are applied to the two types of research. These differences are noted at appropriate points throughout this chapter.

✎ Guideline 7.1
Be wary of any source claiming to offer "proof."

There are certain "proofs" in mathematics and other fields that rely on deduction. Stated simply, they start with certain assumptions and derive a solution that must be true *if* the assumptions are correct. Also, there are certain everyday "facts" that we can probably all agree on as being true. For instance, all people who even briefly look into the matter would probably agree with the "fact" that more voters in California are registered as Democrats than are registered as Republicans. However, when we study complex human behavior, we almost always have at least some degree of uncertainty regarding important principles and theories. Often, we usually have *more uncertainty* than *certainty*.

Note that decisions on how to gather information on a particular topic vary from researcher to researcher. The first decision is whether to use a qualitatively oriented or quantitatively oriented approach (or a combination of both). Quantitatively oriented researchers tend to start with well-defined plans for generating information and reducing it to statistics. Qualitatively oriented researchers start with less well-defined plans. They are more likely to make changes in their methodology (e.g., changes in the wording of questions for an interview as they gain insights from participants). Given that there are two fundamentally different approaches to conducting research on a topic (both of which are generally recognized as valuable), you can see that it will be difficult to arrive at a single "truth" about a topic examined with the two approaches.

Even among quantitative researchers, there are often differences of opinion on how to interpret basic statistical results. For example, one researcher might interpret a particular correlation coefficient as representing a "strong" relationship while another might interpret it as "very strong."

Many of the reasons for uncertainty will be covered in the next five guidelines, which cover issues regarding sampling (identifying a sample of participants from a population) and measurement (measuring participants' traits).

In the face of this inherent uncertainty, we should make decisions based on principles and theories that seem *most likely* to be true. In fact, this is the primary reason for conducting literature reviews: to synthesize the often contradictory literature on a topic to arrive at defensible conclusions regarding what seems to be true based on the *body of research* (both quantitative and qualitative) on a topic. Note that the validity of theories, which should be carefully considered when writing literature reviews, should be assessed on the basis of the extent to which research seems to confirm.

Box 7A *The major purpose for preparing a literature review.*

> The major purpose for preparing a literature review is to synthesize literature in order to arrive at defensible conclusions in the face of the inherent uncertainty of the results reported in both qualitative and quantitative research reports.

Instead of using the words "prove" or "proof," most researchers hedge by using wording that indicates uncertainty. In fact, most will hedge even when there is seemingly overwhelming evidence that something is true because they know that the largest advances in science have been made when a concept or principle that was almost universally regarded as being true (e.g., the world is flat) has been shown to be untrue. Box 7B shows examples of how carefully worded statements are made in the face of varying degrees of uncertainty.

Box 7B *Expressions indicating degrees of certainty in the absence of proof.*

Degree of Certainty	Sample Expressions	Sample Topic
Almost absolutely certain	Almost without exception, the medical community believes… The evidence from all major studies overwhelmingly supports the finding that…	The effects of cigarette smoking on health (i.e., it is harmful to health).
Close to certain	Few who have reviewed the body of literature on XYZ would disagree with the contention that…	Topics will vary.
Fair degree of certainty	Recent studies seem to confirm the major premises of the ABC theory. Specifically, …	Topics will vary.
Rather uncertain	Although the single study that supports this finding is strong methodologically, additional studies and replications are needed before reaching firm conclusions regarding…	Topics will vary.
Very uncertain	The results of an initial pilot study suggest that… Some very preliminary evidence leads us to believe…	The effects of a new educational virtual reality computer program tested with sixteen students without a control group.

As a general rule, give higher evaluations to the conclusions stated in literature in which the statements indicating the degree of certainty are consistent with the amount and quality of the evidence analyzed and presented. Beware of researchers who claim to offer "proof."

When you write your review, you may want to refer back to Box 7B and consider how to phrase the conclusions you reach in your synthesis of the literature. In other words, you should express your conclusions carefully to indicate the extent to which you are certain of them.

✍ Guideline 7.2

Research is almost always flawed by inadequate samples.

Quantitative researchers emphasize the desirability of identifying all members of a population of interest (such as all students majoring in economics in the United States) and drawing a random sample (such as drawing names out of a hat). Often, there are problems in identifying all members of a population (e.g., contacting all universities and colleges in the United States to get the names and contact information for all economics majors would be a daunting task). When this is true, quantitative researchers tend to use a population (such as the students majoring in economics in *one* university) that is more limited than the one they want to study. In a more limited setting, it is often possible to draw names at random. However, participation in studies is almost always voluntary, and in most samples, at least some (and sometimes many) of those selected at random refuse to participate. This leads to what is known as a "biased sample," which might easily lead to "biased results."

Qualitative researchers prefer "purposive sampling" over random sampling. They establish a general purpose for their research (such as identifying the factors that lead minority women to be successful in engineering) and then seek out and select participants who are likely to provide useful information for achieving their purpose. Qualitative researchers stress gaining a thorough understanding of their particular participants by using intensive measurement methods such as extensive interviews. In general, qualitative researchers are less concerned with generalizing to populations than are quantitative researchers. Still, a reviewer of research should be concerned with whether the search for a purposive sample was conducted with care and whether the results were tilted in one direction or another by the refusal of some to participate in qualitative studies.

Give lower evaluations to quantitative and qualitative research reports in which the researchers used individuals who just happened to be available as their research participants. This is called an "accidental" or "convenience" sample. Such a sample does not allow a quantitative researcher to generalize to a population. It also is counterproductive for qualitative researchers who need particular types of participants to achieve their research purposes.

✥ Guideline 7.3

Be cautious when a body of literature has a common sampling flaw.

It is not unusual to find an entire body of research literature on a topic to have a common sampling flaw. For instance, most research in the social and behavioral sciences is conducted by professors who often have limited resources. As a result, a large proportion of studies are conducted with college/university students who volunteer to participate. This provides us with no knowledge of how nonvolunteers would respond or how individuals who are not students would respond.

When there is a common sampling flaw in all (or most) of the studies being reviewed, this should be pointed out in the literature review as a weakness in the body of the research literature on the topic.

✥ Guideline 7.4

Research is almost always flawed by inadequate measures.

Measures in research (often called "instrumentation") vary greatly from highly structured (such as multiple-choice achievement tests or personality scales) to highly unstructured (such as loosely structured, free-flowing interviews). In addition, some traits are inherently easier to measure (such as first-grade math achievement) than others (such as proneness to engage in violent behavior). However, even the most objectively measured and easy-to-measure traits are measured with imperfect instruments or under imperfect circumstances. For instance, (a) some first graders taking a math test might be ill on the day the test is administered, (b) some might be distracted, (c) while others might not understand the test directions or understand the nature of the time limits for testing, and so on. In addition, because of questionable judgment on the part of the test maker, a given test might not include one or more important math concepts or might have poorly phrased math word problems.

Consider this example: A researcher is planning a study on the incidence of driving under the influence (DUI) of alcohol. Box 7C lists some measurement approaches that might be used. Note that each has drawbacks that might potentially flaw the results of the study.

Ideally, a study on DUI should consider a number of potentially related variables (e.g., risk-taking propensities, self-esteem, self-control, addiction to alcohol) that potentially might tie the DUI behavior to one or more theories. Note that there also would be no perfect way to measure any of these other variables.

↳ Guideline 7.5

Consider the reliability of measures used in research.

Reliability refers to the consistency of results. Researchers often address this issue, which you should consider when evaluating the overall dependability of the results.

Qualitative researchers, for instance, often report the extent to which two or more independent individuals identified the same themes when analyzing participants' responses to loosely structured interviews. Their agreement is often expressed as a percentage.

Quantitative researchers (who tend to use objectively scored measures) often report on reliability using correlation coefficients (ranging from 0.00 for no reliability to 1.00 for perfect reliability).[1] Often, you will find

---

[1] Quantitative researchers often report coefficient alpha (α), which is a type of correlation coefficient, to indicate "reliability." It indicates the extent to which the individual items in a measure yield similar results, that is, yield results that agree with each other. (This is somewhat analogous to reporting the extent to which researchers in qualitative studies agree with each other.)

reliabilities ranging from about 0.65 to 0.85 reported for measures used in research, indicating moderate to high reliability.

Other things being equal, give higher evaluations to studies in which the reliability of the measures have been established and reported at acceptable levels such as 80% or higher agreement in qualitative studies or correlation coefficients of 0.65 or higher in quantitative studies.

Box 7C *Approaches to measurement in a study on DUI.*

Approach	Drawback
Questionnaire with objective-type items asking about DUI behavior in the past	Respondents might not be willing to admit to the behavior and may give socially desirable responses even if responses are anonymous.
	Respondents might interpret "under the influence" in various ways. The questionnaire might provide a definition, which would help reduce the problem.
Brief structured interviews	Same drawbacks as the first approach except that responses will not be anonymous, increasing the possibility of failing to admit to DUI behavior.
In-depth interviews	If rapport is established, respondents might be more likely to admit to DUI behavior.
	Subjectivity required to interpret and summarize results across a group of respondents may lead to errors in analysis.
Direct observation	Subjects might behave differently if they know they are being observed (such as when leaving a bar).
	The sample of observations will probably be limited (e.g., cannot follow subjects everywhere; subjects might drink in private).
Questioning significant others	They might be unwilling to "squeal" on their significant others.
	They might not be with the subjects at appropriate times (e.g., parents not going out with subjects on their dates).
Examining criminal records available to the public	Would yield information on *only* those who were driving under the influence *and* were stopped by police *and* were charged *and* convicted.

ᖆ Guideline 7.6

Consider the validity of measures used in research.

Validity refers to the extent to which an instrument measures what it is supposed to measure. Note that a measure can be highly reliable without being valid. For instance, consider an extreme example that makes this point clear. If a researcher tried to measure the cognitive skills of legal immigrants passing through the U.S.–Mexican border with a series of questions asked in English, those with limited English-language skills would understandably perform poorly. Asking these immigrants the same questions repeatedly would likely yield consistent (i.e., reliable) results. Yet, the results would be of extremely dubious validity because the questions were posed in a language with which the immigrants were not fluent. Hence, when evaluating a measure, it is not sufficient to consider only its reliability.

Most professionals in measurement would agree that most widely used measures have higher reliability than validity. It is beyond the scope of this book to explore the many approaches and controversies concerning how to estimate the validity of a measure. However, even if you have not taken a course in tests and measurements, you can look for obvious flaws (e.g., asking questions about sensitive measures without anonymity and/or without establishing rapport with the participants) when you evaluate a research article.

Note that in good scientific reporting, researchers address the issue of the validity of their measures. Often, they use published measures for which you can obtain validity information from the test publisher. Probably as often as not, researchers use measures they have constructed especially for use in their research. You should give lower evaluations to studies in which the researchers fail to provide some evidence of the validity of their measures because in the absence of such evidence, you will often have no basis for judging whether the measures are valid.

Sometimes researchers report the actual wording of questions posed on questionnaires or in interviews. When this is the case, consider the questions carefully. Ask questions such as: Are they clearly stated? Could they be misinterpreted? Do they cover the topic thoroughly? Are they worded in such a way that they might influence the respondents to answer in one way rather than another? Box 7D shows examples of defective interview/questionnaire items. Such items lower the validity of the measures.

Box 7D *A sample of defective interview/questionnaire items.*

Item	Defect
As you may know, the President of the United States believes that X is greater than Y. Do you think that X is greater than Y?	Citing the opinion of an authority might sway the opinions of the respondents to the question.
Are you confident that the economy of the United States is improving? __ Yes __ No	The item fails to allow for degrees of opinion. For instance, it does not provide a choice for someone who is "fairly confident" but not sure enough to respond simply "yes" or "no."
When is the last time you hit your child with your hand?	The question assumes that a parent engaged in this behavior. The question is suitable only if the parents have been prescreened, and the researcher already knows that all have hit their children with their hands.
During your career, how many times have you been ill enough to miss two or more consecutive days of work?	For adults, the timeframe is too long. For instance, an older worker might not be able to remember how many times this happened. Note that it is better to use a shorter timeframe such as "in the last year."
Have you used any tobacco products during the last seven days? __ Yes __ No	As an anonymous question, it is satisfactory. However, it is unsatisfactory if it is administered to school children who will be handing the questionnaires to their teachers because students might not be willing to admit to the behavior.

⤷ Guideline 7.7

Consider the authors' self-critique of their own research methods.

In good scientific writing, researchers point out the major flaws in their own methodology. Typically, these are flaws that the researchers could not overcome because of limited resources such as time, access to participants, and so on. Very often, these are referred to as "limitations" and are usually discussed briefly near the end of research reports in the Discussion section. Researchers often will also point out major methodological strengths of their studies—especially if they were the first to have these strengths (e.g., the first study on a topic that used a random sample from a population).

By paying close attention to self-critiques of researchers' methodologies, you will be in a better position to evaluate the research reports you will refer to in your literature review. For instance, if a researcher states that his or her study has a major strength, you might check the other studies you have collected to see if they have the same strength. If not, these studies might be weaker than the one claiming a major strength.

↳ Guideline 7.8

Be cautious when a researcher refers to causality.

It is easy to fall into the logical trap of assuming that because A precedes B, A must be the cause of B. By definition, it is true that a cause must occur before its effect appears. However, not every variable that occurs first is necessarily a cause. Here is a simple illustration: Someone notices that students in a particular first-grade classroom, on average, are high achievers in reading. The person also notices that the classroom has a large number of books that were available to the students from the beginning of first grade. Did the large number of books *cause* the high reading achievement? It is not possible to know because many other variables also preceded their achievement. Some examples are: having a very well-qualified teacher assigned to the class, having self-selection (by their parents) of high-potential students to the class, having an effective computer-assisted reading instruction program available in the classroom, and so on.

The study of causality is the source of a major divide between quantitatively oriented and qualitatively oriented researchers. To study causality, quantitatively oriented researchers prefer random assignment to treatment groups and attempt to control extraneous variables. Thus, in the example we have been considering, half of the students would be selected at random to learn reading in a classroom with many books while the remaining ones would be taught reading in a classroom with few books. The researcher would try to establish equality between the two settings on other variables such as the qualifications of the teachers and the availability of other resources such as computer-assisted reading instruction programs that might also affect achievement in reading.

Qualitative researchers, on the other hand, eschew random assignment.

Instead, they take an in-depth look at their participants through intensive interviews, open-ended questionnaires, observations, and so on. Note that self-reports can be difficult to interpret when attempting to identify causal variables not only because participants might not tell the truth about certain aspects of their lives, but they might not have the self-insights to understand why they do what they do (i.e., the cause of their behavior). Thus, a group of juvenile inmates in jail might be interviewed by a qualitative researcher to study the causes of their delinquent behavior. It is the qualitatively oriented researcher's job to question the participants in such a way that the researcher ferrets out information on causation even if the participants are not aware of it or able to verbalize it directly. This can be a daunting task.

If you will be writing a literature review on a topic relating to causation, you should carefully evaluate the evidence presented in research reports to determine the credibility of various purported causal explanations that are offered by researchers.[2]

ᕂ Guideline 7.9
Assess the strength of trends across studies when evaluating literature.

Because it is safe to assume that all research is flawed, it is important to consider the trends across the body of research on a topic and give greater emphasis to the methodologically stronger studies than to weaker ones when writing your review. If the vast majority of studies on a topic has a particular kind of result, while only a slim minority has a different kind of result, give more emphasis to the majority while noting the minority in your literature review. The exception to this principle is if the slim minority clearly has used superior research techniques and presents arguments that are more consistently logical and related to appropriate theories. In this case, you might emphasize the minority while pointing out the flaws of the majority.

---

[2] Like many other issues in this chapter, only the basics of this topic are covered. If you will be writing a literature review for an advanced purpose such as a master's thesis, you should take courses in research methods, statistics, and tests and measurements before undertaking the task of writing a review. On the other hand, for undergraduates who have not taken such coursework, this chapter provides general guidance on many of the basics that should be considered.

↳ Guideline 7.10

Recognize the limitations of significance testing.

Quantitatively oriented researchers typically conduct significance tests. As a result, you will read statements such as "the mean (average) for Group A is significantly higher than the mean for Group B ($p < .05$)."[3] Saying that it is *significantly higher* is equivalent to saying it is *reliably higher*. It is *not* equivalent to saying that the difference is large. In other words, a researcher is saying that a reliable difference has been detected—*not* that the difference is large or important.

Because this concept may be difficult to understand at first, consider this example: Suppose that a disgruntled employee decides that he will clock in to work exactly 30 seconds late each day. Because management is strict about punctuality and the other workers value and enjoy their jobs, the other workers clock in before or just on time. This happens day after day for months on end. At some point, a large enough sample of days would be observed that a significance test would declare the difference in clock-in times between the disgruntled employee and the other employees to be statistically significant *just because it is a reliable phenomenon*—not because the difference (30 seconds) is large enough to be of any practical consequence.

This is an important guideline because many researchers who did not major in statistics but conduct research in their content areas are unaware of it. Thus, it is not uncommon to find researchers discussing their "statistically significant" results as though they were large enough to be of practical significance. One way you can avoid falling into the trap they are unwittingly setting is to consider the raw statistics that underlie the significance tests. For instance, if two means are significantly different, examine the values of the means and consider by how many points they differ and whether that amount of difference is of any practical concern or has practical implications.

---

[3] As you may know, "$p < .05$" indicates that there are only five chances in 100 that the researcher is in error in making the statement that the difference is statistically significant.

Concluding Comments

This chapter presents only a brief overview of some of the basics for evaluating qualitative and quantitative research. Admittedly, you will be at a handicap if you have not previously taken and mastered the material in courses in research methods, statistics, and tests and measurements. However, you will find that many research reports published in academic journals are clearly written and provide enough context and self-criticism to keep you from getting too far astray in your evaluation and interpretation of them.

Exercise for Chapter 7

1. Have any of your peers, colleagues, or instructors ever stated that a study "proves" something? If so, briefly describe what he or she said. In light of this chapter, would you be cautious about believing such a statement? Explain.

2. According to this chapter, what is the major purpose for preparing a literature review?

3. What do quantitative researchers emphasize when sampling that qualitative researchers do *not* emphasize?

4. Name an example of a common sampling flaw.

5. Under Guideline 7.4, this statement is made: "…some traits are inherently easier to measure…than others.…" Name a trait other than the ones mentioned in this chapter that you think is inherently *difficult* to measure.

6. Briefly explain why a highly reliable measuring instrument can be invalid.

7. According to this chapter, should you be surprised to find that the author of a research report points out weaknesses in his or her own research methodology?

8. To study causality, what do quantitative researchers prefer to do?

9. According to this chapter, it is safe to assume that all research is flawed. Because of this, what is important for you to do?

10. If a difference is statistically significant, is it necessarily large? If not, what does the fact that a difference is statistically significant tell you?

11. According to this chapter, should you expect most research reports published in academic journals to be clearly written?

Chapter 8

Planning and Writing the First Draft

At this point, you should have collected the literature relevant to your topic, read it and made notes, and evaluated the literature that reports the results of research. Now you should begin planning and writing your first draft.

☙ Guideline 8.1

Before preparing an outline, review your notes and group them according to content.

Grouping by content is often superior to putting sources in chronological order unless the primary intent of your review is to synthesize information on the history of some topic.[1] Thus, for a literature review of variables associated with investment strategies, you might group together those that deal with gender differences. In another group, you might have those that deal with age differences in investment strategies. In yet another, you might group those that name and define various strategies. Looking at your groupings should help you prepare an outline for your literature review.

☙ Guideline 8.2

When beginning to build a topic outline, consider the order in which other writers have presented material on your topic.

---

[1] Even for an historical review, you should group according to content within each historical time period.

For instance, if your topic is regional differences in voting patterns in national elections, consider the various ways and the order in which material was presented by previous authors. Did they begin by defining what they mean by voting patterns? Did they define the regions of interest to them? Did they provide an historical overview and, if so, where did they do so? Near the beginning? Near the end? Noticing patterns such as these should give you some ideas on how to organize your outline.[2]

ꙮ Guideline 8.3

Consider your first topic outline as a tentative one that is subject to change.

This guideline is suggested for two reasons. First, if you are considering a substantial amount of material on a topic, you might feel overwhelmed as to how to organize it. Considering the outline for it as only tentative and subject to change may make you feel more comfortable and overcome initial writer's block. After all, it is only a tentative first stab—not the final product. Second, you will be more willing to change it after showing it to others (such as your instructor) for feedback.

Unless your instructor requires that you strictly follow an approved outline, feel free to change it (by adding, subtracting, or rearranging topics) during the writing process. Good writers often change directions several times during the process of writing an important work.

It is important to put your outline in writing. While highly skilled writers sometimes can work effectively without a written outline, it is unwise for most writers to use only a mental outline.

Example 8.3.1 shows a topic outline. Note that it starts with a general introduction. In a thesis or dissertation, the introduction might be a separate chapter (usually chapter 1) from the literature review (usually chapter 2). In journal articles, the introduction is typically integrated with the literature review, with references to literature being referred to as early as the first

---

[2] Note that even a brief literature review that precedes a report of original research will have some type of organization even if it does not have subheadings for major content groupings.

sentence. Check with your instructor as to which arrangement he or she prefers.

Example 8.3.1

A topic outline for a literature review:[3]

Title: The Effects of Praise on Children's Intrinsic Motivation

General Introduction to the Topic

Defining Praise and Motivation

Two Contrasting Views

Praise Enhances Intrinsic Motivation

   –Beneficial mechanisms

Praise Undermines Intrinsic Motivation

   –Detrimental mechanisms

Conceptual Variables Influencing the Effects of Praise on Intrinsic Motivation

Sincerity

Performance Attributions

   –Attributions as mediators

   –Ability versus effort praise

   –Person versus process praise

   –Overview of attributions

Perceived Autonomy

   –Praise as extrinsic reward

   –Informational versus controlling aspects of praise

   –Gender differences in perceived autonomy

   –Overview of autonomy

Standards and Expectations

   –The moderating function of standards and expectations

   –Gender differences in familiarity of standards and expectations

   –Overview of standards and expectations

Summary of Conceptual Variables

A Cultural Caveat

Directions for Future Research

Appropriate Control Conditions

Appropriate Dependent Measures

Appropriate Manipulations

Summary and Conclusions

---

[3] This outline is loosely based on the work of Henderlong & Lepper (2002).

Note that in the outline in Example 8.3.1, the main headings are in bold, the second-level headings are in italics, and the third-level headings are indented with dashes in front of them. Any arrangement of this sort is acceptable if it is only a working topic outline for your use while writing. If you must submit an outline to an instructor, you might want to use the method commonly taught in English composition courses: Roman numerals for first-level headings, capital letters of the alphabet for second-level headings, and so on.

When writing your literature review, consult with the recommended style manual for your university or for your field of study for guidance on how to format the levels of headings. For example, the *Publication Manual of the American Psychological Association* has specific guidelines for various levels of headings, some of which are shown in Example 8.3.2.

Example 8.3.2
Some levels of headings from the Publication Manual of the American Psychological Association:

Level one:

Centered Uppercase and Lowercase Heading

Level two:

Centered, Italicized, Uppercase and Lowercase Heading

Level three:

Flush Left, Italicized, Uppercase and Lowercase Side Heading[4]

ꙮ Guideline 8.4

Consider filling in your outline with brief notes (including unique identifiers) before beginning to write your review.

Guideline 5.5 in Chapter 5 suggests that you give each piece of literature a unique identifier such as the surname of the first author. You can start filling in your outline by writing notes within the outline that indicate what material will be presented under each heading (and subheading) and which sources will be used. This is done in Example 8.4.1, where the notes

---

[4] American Psychological Association (2001, p. 113).

are shown in smaller type in brackets below some of the early topics in the outline in Example 8.3.1.

Example 8.4.1

A topic outline for a literature review with notes and identifiers on what to cover and the sources to be used. Notes and identifiers are shown in brackets:

The Effects of Praise on Children's Intrinsic Motivation

General Introduction to the Topic

> [Topic is important because praise is so widely used: Smith & Stall; Doe.
>
> Teachers' and parents' beliefs on the importance of praise: Doe; Brown.
>
> Failure of parents and teachers to recognize that different schedules of praise may have different effects: Blackwell & Wright; Logan; Manchester & Lake.]

Defining Praise and Motivation

> [Use Black's definition of "praise."
>
> Define "intrinsic motivation" and "extrinsic motivation" separately by paraphrasing definitions in Doe & Barnes.
>
> Stress that this review is on *intrinsic* motivation only. Justify this restriction using Noble & Smith's rationale. Mention Jackson's theory, which supports Noble & Smith.]

Two Contrasting Views

Praise Enhances Intrinsic Motivation

> [Describe circumstances and studies that support enhancement: Franklin & James; Smith & Smith; Jackson, Washington, & Adams.
>
> Outline theory that explains this phenomenon: Blackwell, Wright, & Logan; Honeywell; Langly & Sears.
>
> Provide details on Doe's classic study with attention to circumstances when enhancement was found in her study. Mention replications: Bruce, Harris, & Corwin; Moeller; Brahm & Lake; Doe.]

Notice in Example 8.4.1, the reviewer is making the topic outline more concrete by adding cryptic notes. Also notice that several of the notes have more than one source. For instance, the works of Smith & Small *and* Doe will be cited for the first note made in the outline. In addition, it is important to notice that a given source may appear in several places within the outline. For example, Doe is cited for the first note as well as in the last one in the example.[5] This repetition of sources in various places in the outline occurs because it is an outline built around *topics*—not around individual pieces of literature. Thus, a work such as Doe's may have information that is relevant to more than one topic within the outline.

If they are readily available when you make your cryptic notes within your topic outline, relevant page numbers should be included.

⅏ Guideline 8.5

Establish the importance of the topic that you are reviewing in the introductory paragraphs of your review.

The word "importance" may be used as illustrated in Example 8.5.1, in which literature is cited to justify the assertion that a topic is important.

Example 8.5.1

A statement of importance from the introduction to a literature review:

The importance of values in social work is indisputable, for values represent a fundamental working element in social work practice and ethics (Bartlett, 1958;...Loewenberg & Dolgoff, 1992). Social work values embody social workers' preferred views of people, what they prefer for people, and how they work with people (Levy, 1973). Values guide social work practice, and, ultimately, express social workers' commitments to action.[6]

The importance of a topic can also be established by citing the statistics on the numbers of people (or percentage of people) affected by the topic.[7] This is illustrated in Example 8.5.2. Even though it involves reporting statistics, this approach can be used by both those writing qualitatively oriented and those writing quantitatively oriented literature reviews.

---

[5] Of course, if two different authors have the same surname, add first names (such as Doe, John and Doe, Monica) or years of publication (such as Doe [2000] and Doe [2002]). Using years of publication is desirable if the author has written more than one source that will be cited in the review.

[6] Pinto (2002, p. 85).

[7] A topic might be justified in terms of the seriousness of the consequences for a *small* percentage of people. For instance, a life-threatening disease that affects only a fraction of one percent of the population is an important topic because of its potentially devastating effects.

Example 8.5.2

Importance of a topic (ADHD) is established by citing statistics:

In the last decade, there has been a rapid rise in the reported prevalence rates of ADHD. Robinson, Sclar, Skaer, and Galin (1999) examined the National Ambulatory Medical Care Survey data for the years 1990 through 1995. They found that the number of office-based visits documenting a diagnosis of ADHD increased from 947,208 in 1990 to 2,357,833 in 1995. This increase in diagnosis was matched with a 2.9-fold increase in the number of ADHD individuals prescribed stimulant medication.[8]

The U.S. Census Bureau, which can be accessed via the Internet at www.census.gov/, is a good source of statistics on many matters. Example 8.5.3 illustrates this point.

Example 8.5.3

Example of establishing the importance of a topic using Census Bureau statistics:

Almost 30% of all children are currently being raised in single-parent homes and have a nonresident parent (U.S. Census Bureau, 1999).[9]

↳ Guideline 8.6

Avoid vague references to statistics—especially in the first paragraph of your review.

Many literature reviews *inappropriately* begin with sentences such as those shown in Example 8.6.1. They are inappropriate unless they are followed shortly afterwards with specific statistics that support them. Without statistical support (even in qualitative reviews) nonstatistical statements about statistical matters cause insightful readers to wince at the thought that you are giving your personal impressions of what statistics *might* reveal instead of being a careful researcher who has collected relevant statistics from the literature. (If you insist on *not* following this guideline, you should at least make a statement to this effect: "It is *my general impression* that people are increasingly interested in....)

---

[8] Purdie, Hattie, & Carroll (2002, p. 63).
[9] Bloomer, Sipe, & Ruedt (2002, p. 77).

Example 8.6.1

Statements with vague references to statistics (inappropriate unless they are followed by specific supporting statistics with sources):

In recent years, economists increasingly have become interested in the XYZ theory of economic trends and have....[Note: In which recent years? How does the author know there is an increase? What is the size of the increase?]

More and more teachers are facing the dilemma of integrating special-needs children into their classrooms without adequate training on techniques and....[Note: How many are "more and more"? What is the source of this vague quantity?]

⅏ Guideline 8.7

Provide specific definitions of major variables early in the literature review.

Definitions of major variables are essential to avoid miscommunication between you and your readers. Also, differences in how various researchers define variables may help to explain discrepancies in results across studies, which is an issue that should be addressed in your review. Specifically, those researchers using one type of definition may be consistently finding different results than those using another type, a possibility that you should consider while writing your review. For instance, if one researcher defines "physical child abuse" as "any form of physical punishment" while another researcher defines it to exclude mild forms of spanking with an open hand, you would expect differences between the results of the two studies.

It is acceptable (and sometimes desirable) to use a previously published definition as long as you cite its source, as is done in Example 8.7.1. The first sentence in the example provides the definition while the two sentences that follow help to clarify the definition by citing some characteristics of those who fit it. If there is a previously published definition that prevails in the literature you are reviewing, it is a good idea to use it as your definition also for the sake of consistency in communications—unless you think it is a flawed definition, in which case you should point out its flaws and offer your own.

Example 8.7.1

A definition attributed to another source (an acceptable practice):

Job burnout has been defined as a syndrome characterized by physical and emotional exhaustion resulting from excessive demands on the energy, strength, and resources of the worker (Spicuzza & De Voe, 1982). Workers who suffer from job burnout are less effective on the job. They are more likely to be emotionally exhausted, depersonalize their clients, feel less personal accomplishment, and feel less commitment to their occupation (Miller et al., 1995).[10]

⚡ Guideline 8.8

Write an essay that moves logically from one point to another. Do not write a string of annotations.

An annotation is a summary of a piece of literature. Most academic literature (especially journal articles) has already been annotated, and the annotations have been published. As a reviewer of literature, it is your job to make an original contribution—not just annotate literature again—and write an essay that moves logically from topic to topic. References should be cited as needed, and a given reference may be cited repeatedly in different parts of your essay, as needed.

An essay will result if you build and follow a *topic* outline (see Guidelines 8.1 through 8.3). In short, your narrative should move from topic to topic as indicated on your outline—not from the work of one author to the work of another author.

⚡ Guideline 8.9

When they are available, use more than one reference to support a point you make. However, do not cite very long strings of references for a single point.

Example 8.9.1, in which two sources are cited for a single point, illustrates this guideline.

---

[10] Franze, Foster, Abbott-Shim, McCarty, & Lambert (2002, p. 259).

Example 8.9.1

An example of citing more than one source for a given point:

Interest groups purchase advertising space in mass media to explain their views because it is an economical means of communicating their message to the general public, and they believe that their ads have had an effect on the general public (Kollman, 1998; Loomis & Sexton, 1995).[11]

On the other hand, do *not* cite very long strings of references for a single point. Instead, cite a limited number of the more important ones, starting with "e.g.," as illustrated in Example 8.9.2.

Example 8.9.2

An example of using "e.g." when there are many sources for a single point:

The XYZ theory has wide support (e.g., Smith, 2001; Jones, 2002).

If you want to stress that there are a very large number of supporting studies (and/or theoretical literature), you can also make a statement such as the one in Example 8.9.3, in which the number of studies is mentioned but only a few are cited.

Example 8.9.3

An example of using "see especially" when there are many sources for a single point and mention is made of the number of studies that have such support:

The XYZ theory has wide support, with 14 studies published within the last decade that provide supporting data (see especially: Smith, 2001; Jones, 2002).

A major exception to this guideline sometimes occurs when students are writing literature reviews for theses and dissertations, which are, in essence, long-term take-home tests (i.e., performance tasks). Students writing theses and dissertations may be asked to cite *all* relevant literature as a test of their ability to locate it and appropriately cite it. Occasionally, this may also be required for a class paper or senior project for the same reason. Consult with your instructor for further clarification on this issue.

---

[11] Hunter (2002, p. 390).

⮎ Guideline 8.10

Use quotations sparingly. Instead write the literature review using your own words.

Strings of quotations will result in a paper that is uneven in style. Even more important, as a reviewer of literature, you are expected to make an original contribution by recasting the literature you have read in your own words so that your entire narrative makes sense logically and is cohesive.

The main exception to this guideline is when an idea is expressed so aptly that its impact or intensity achieved through the use of rhetorical devices would be lost in paraphrase. Arguably, the impact of the quotation in Example 8.10.1 would be lost if it were merely paraphrased.

Example 8.10.1

A quotation whose impact might be lost in paraphrase:

Willis (1994), for example, writes that "to succeed as an athlete can be to fail as a woman, because she has, in certain symbolic ways, become a man" (p. 36).[12]

Be especially cautious about beginning your literature review with a direct quotation from the literature. Remember, it is *your* literature review, and it makes sense for you to begin it in your own words. An exception is when a quotation is exceedingly apt and very clearly sets the stage for what you are about to write. In scientific writing, there rarely is a quotation that meets the standards for this exception.

⮎ Guideline 8.11

Explicitly state what you think are reasonable conclusions based on the literature for each major subtopic that you cover.

It is not sufficient merely to present the evidence from the literature without discussing at least the major conclusions that you think are supported by it, as illustrated in Example 8.11.1.

---

[12] Christopherson, Janning, & McConnell (2002, p. 172).

Example 8.11.1

A tentative conclusion based on the literature:

In sum, this review of the literature on XYZ clearly suggests that the ABC model is more predictive of future alcohol behavior than the DEF model given the nature of the preliminary evidence published to date.

Remember to avoid using the words "prove" and "proof" when following this guideline. See Guideline 7.1 in Chapter 7.

Note that Guideline 8.11 should be followed in conjunction with the next three guidelines.

☙ Guideline 8.12

Consider theories and/or models when reaching conclusions.

This guideline is suggested because conclusions regarding theories and models are likely to be more important than conclusions about simple factual matters because they have more implications. Example 8.11.1 above illustrates a statement that refers to models.

If you reach a conclusion that a widely accepted theory may be flawed or invalid, reread your literature review to be certain that you have sufficient supporting material to reach such a conclusion (one that runs contrary to prevailing opinion). Also, check to see that you have included all the relevant literature. If so, then feel free to make statements that run counter to the mainstream.

☙ Guideline 8.13

Critique the research you cite, which will help you show your readers why you have reached particular conclusions.

Close examination of the literature on almost any complex topic will reveal at least minor contradictions (and sometimes major ones) in the results of the research on the topic. In general, consider basing conclusions on the studies with superior research methodologies. (Chapter 7 provides a number of guidelines for evaluating research.)

Note that if you fail to point out that one research study is superior to another, your readers are likely to assume that both are about equal in their research methodology. If they are not equal in your opinion but you do not say so, you may be misleading your readers. Example 8.13.1 shows a potentially misleading statement about two groups of contradictory studies followed by one that differentiates between the two groups in terms of methodology.

Example 8.13.1

A statement that misleads because no differentiation is made between studies:

Several studies (Doe, 2002; Smith, 2001) provide support for the contention that XYZ is correct. In contrast, other studies (Jones, 2001; Long, 2002) fail to support this contention.

A statement that makes distinctions based on research methodology:

While several studies (Doe, 2002; Smith, 2001) provide support for the contention that XYZ is correct, others (Jones, 2001; Long, 2002) fail to support this contention. It is important to note that the latter studies used more representative samples than the former, lending credence to the conclusion that XYZ is possibly incorrect.

Example 8.13.2 shows a brief part of the conclusion from a literature review in which they conclude that goal-setting theory is supported by the research literature. Notice that they point out flaws in studies that fail to support the theory.

Example 8.13.2

A conclusion about goal-setting theory that is based on a critique of research methods:

The effects of goal setting are very reliable. Failures to replicate them are usually due to errors, such as not matching the goal to the performance measure, not providing feedback, not getting goal commitment....[13]

---

[13] Locke & Latham (2002, p. 714).

⤷ Guideline 8.14

Point out gaps in the literature, explain why they are important, and mention them in your conclusions.

The conclusions that you reach at the end of your literature review may be especially tentative if there are no (or only a few) studies on some issues that are highly relevant to your topic. Also, point out why the gap hinders our understanding of the phenomenon. This is illustrated in Example 8.14.1.[14]

Example 8.14.1

A statement about a gap in the literature and its importance:

With the exception of research into the influence of sibling smoking status on youth imitation, few studies have examined the role of nonparental family members in smoking onset. This may be a fruitful area for investigation because the extended family plays a more salient role in the lives of children in some nonwhite cultures.[23,24] Extended family members…may engage in meaningful anti-smoking socialization or may contribute to teen smoking through the same mechanisms as parents and siblings.[15]

Concluding Comments

By reading a large number of well-crafted literature reviews (such as those that typically appear in journals), you will see a variety of structures and techniques used to introduce a topic, critically summarize what is known about it, write a cohesive essay that synthesizes literature, and reach defensible conclusions. The guidelines in this chapter show you only the major techniques for structuring and writing a literature review.

If you have carefully built a topic outline as described at the beginning of this chapter and followed the remaining guidelines, you should have a suitable *first draft* of your literature review. In the next two chapters, we will consider some additional refinements and niceties that you might use to

---

[14] Note that superscripts 23 and 24 in example 8.14.1 refer to references in the original review that support the statement about the gap. Superscript 15 identifies the reference for the quotation shown in the example.
[15] Kegler et al. (2002, p. 475).

improve your first draft. The old truism deserves mention here: The key to effective writing is rewriting.

Exercise for Chapter 8

1. If you have already gathered literature, name several of the groupings you will use. If you have not gathered literature yet, name some groupings you anticipate that you will use. See Guideline 8.1.

2. Notice that "Defining Praise and Motivation" is the second major heading in Example 8.3.1. What major terms do you anticipate defining in your literature review? Will you define them in a separate section with its own major heading such as in the example, *or* will you integrate the definitions into your narrative (defining each when it is first introduced)?

3. Examine Example 8.3.1. Excluding the title, how many levels of headings are shown? How can you distinguish among the levels in the example?

4. Have you been assigned a style manual that covers formatting matters such as levels of headings and other matters regarding presentation of material? If so, name it. If not, will you use a style manual? If yes, which one?

5. Examine Model Literature Review 3 on religion-accommodative counseling. Read the title and then read the first- and second-level headings (without reading the text). To what extent do the headings help you get a sense of what is covered in the review? In your opinion, is the review long enough to justify the number of headings and subheadings the authors used?

6. What is your opinion on Guideline 8.4? Do you plan to follow it? Why? Why not?

7. Notice that some authors' names appear in more than one place in the outline in Example 8.4.1. According to the material in this chapter, why does this occur?

8. If you have access to the Internet, go to www.census.gov/ and explore the Web site, looking for statistics that are relevant to your topic. Very briefly describe your findings here.

9. According to this chapter, what is wrong with starting a review with a statement such as "Each year, more adolescents drop out of high school, which increases their odds of never finding a well-paying job."?

10. According to this chapter, is it acceptable to cite and use a previously published definition of a variable you are discussing in your review? Explain.

11. Select one of the variables you will be covering in your literature review. Define it here. Indicate whether it is a draft of the definition *or* a finalized definition.

12. According to this chapter, what are some alternatives to citing a long string of references for a single point?

13. According to this chapter, why should direct quotations be used sparingly in literature reviews?

14. According to this chapter, should writers of literature reviews state their own conclusions drawn from the literature, *or* should they describe the literature in a cohesive essay but "let the facts speak for themselves" instead of stating their own conclusions?

15. According to this chapter, if several research studies are cited but not critiqued, what are readers likely to assume?

16. If you have already searched the literature, are you aware of any important gaps in the research on your topic? If so, very briefly describe them here.

Chapter 9

Revising and Refining the First Draft

Having written your first draft, review it while considering the following guidelines. Usually, it is best to allow at least a couple of days to intervene between finishing the first draft and reviewing it for revision in order for you to be fresh during the revision process.

ᕈ Guideline 9.1

Recheck headings and subheadings. Modify and/or add or delete as necessary.

In the last chapter, you were urged to build a topic outline and make cryptic notes for each of the major headings and subheadings in the outline. Flushing out your notes can create a first draft in which you use the topic headings/subheadings from your outline as the headings/subheadings in your literature review.

As you revise your first draft, consider whether any of the headings/subheadings should be reworded in light of the narrative you wrote. Also, consider whether additional headings/subheadings are needed. For example, you may have quite a bit of material on how participants at various educational levels responded to variables related to your topic. In such a case, consider whether the set of literature might be broken into two or more categories. For instance, instead of using "education" as a single subheading, you might use "high school dropouts" and "high school graduates."

If you find that you have only one piece of literature for each of a number of headings, you might want to combine them so that you can discuss several pieces of literature under one heading.

As a general rule, be generous in the use of headings and subheadings. They help readers understand the organization of your review and follow your transitions from one topic or subtopic to another. Although it is difficult to quantify this matter in the abstract without referring to specific content, a useful guideline might be that there should be at least one heading or subheading for every two double-spaced typewritten pages of your review. Feel free to disregard this guideline if it will create illogical cutting points or transitions.

☙ Guideline 9.2
Check to see that all your paragraphs are straightforward and reasonably short.

Good scientific writing is clear writing. Unlike creative writing, in which one might strive for variety, the purpose of scientific writing is to communicate information clearly and unambiguously. It is perfectly acceptable in scientific writing to write paragraphs that follow the simplest model for paragraph writing: Write a topic sentence first (e.g., "Studies of the use of polygraphs in employment selection in major corporations have had mixed results") and then write sentences that provide details on the topic (e.g., "One of the earliest studies of its use for this purpose [Doe, 1971] showed promising…").

Remember that readers of literature reviews are reading to learn content—not to be entertained. Writing that might be considered pedestrian in a creative writing class may be desirable when writing a literature review. Readers who are interested in the content you are covering will appreciate simple, unpretentious writing that employs straightforward paragraphs.

☙ Guideline 9.3
Check to see that you have used rhetorical questions sparingly.

A rhetorical question is one that the writer answers immediately. Such a question is often used as the topic sentence of a paragraph. Occasional use can provide variety in paragraph beginnings. Too many rhetorical questions, on the other hand, can be distracting. Example 9.3.1 shows the use of a rhetorical question at the beginning of a paragraph. The answer to the question is discussed in the six paragraphs that follow it; only a portion of the first of the six is shown in the example.

Example 9.3.1

A paragraph that begins with a rhetorical question:

Why do people die in famines? This question seems to invite a simple answer, but in fact the answer is the subject of much contention. This is a problem because views on the issue have major implications for policies toward malnourished populations....[1]

☙ Guideline 9.4

Consider using transitional terms to make one paragraph flow from the previous one.

Example 9.4.1 shows the beginning of the first paragraph in a literature review designed to introduce and justify the authors' hypotheses. The beginnings of each of the four subsequent paragraphs are shown in the example. For instructional purposes, transitional terms used by the writer to help readers see how each paragraph flows from the previous one are italicized in bold.

Example 9.4.1

*Portions of a beginning paragraph followed by the beginnings of paragraphs that contain transitional terms (**italicized in bold**)*:

A considerable body of theory suggests that elected public officials in a democracy have reason to pay attention to public opinion. Rational choice theorists, for example, have long argued....

Empirically, ***too***, there is substantial scholarly evidence of rather close connections between citizens' preferences....

---

[1] Loosely based on Hionidou (2002, p. 65).

Moreover, there has been an enormous increase in policy-related polls and surveys of public opinion....

Given this abundance of information about public opinion, most of us would probably *also* expect that politicians would take note of....

Thus, our hypotheses...are the following....[2]

In his book on rhetoric and style in writing, Harris (2003) illustrates the use of transitions. Portions of his statements about them are shown in Box 9A. Note that he advises against the use of too many strong transitions. Box 9B provides many examples of transitional terms. Harris has classified them according to function (e.g., "addition" and "comparison") as well as according to strength (i.e., "milder" and "stronger"). As you revise your first draft, refer to these terms for ideas on how to improve the transitions among the paragraphs on each topic/subtopic within your review. Also, consider whether you have used appropriate ones *within* individual paragraphs.

Box 9A *The use of transitional terms.*[3]

1. Use transitions between paragraphs to signal connections (addition, contrast, and so forth) between idea segments. Use transitions within paragraphs to signal a change from one sentence to another or from one section of the paragraph to another.
2. Use sufficient transitions to provide coherence (holding together, like glue) and continuity (making the thought process easy to follow). Less experienced writers tend to supply too few transitions.
3. Avoid using too many strong transitions. Be careful to avoid littering your writing with *however* and *nevertheless*. Strong transitions should be used sparingly.
4. Transitions become stronger when they are placed at the beginning (or end) of a sentence, milder (or less strong) when they are moved into the sentence. Generally, moving transitions into the sentence is the better choice.

[2] Cook, Barabas, & Page (2002, pp. 237–238).
[3] Harris (2003, p. 35).

115

Box 9B *Transitional terms that can be used to provide coherence.*[4]

	Milder		Stronger	
Addition	a further x	next	additionally	first, second
	also	nor	again	further
	and	other	besides	furthermore
	and then	then	equally important	in addition
	another	too	finally, last	moreover
Comparison	a similar x	just as…so too	comparable	likewise
	another x like		in the same way	similarly
Contrast	and yet	rather	alternatively	nonetheless
	but	still	at the same time	notwithstanding
	but another	though	conversely	on the contrary
	or	yet	even so	on the other
	otherwise		for all that	hand
			however	otherwise
			in contrast	still
			instead	though this may
			nevertheless	be
Time	after	now	at last	immediately
	afterward	recently	at length	meanwhile
	before	shortly	at that time	presently
	earlier	soon	currently	subsequently
	first, second, third	then	eventually	thereafter
	later	today	finally	
	next	tomorrow		
Purpose	because of this x	to do this	for that reason	to this end
			for this purpose	with this object
Place	beyond	nearby	adjacent to	in the front
	here	there	at that point	on the other side
			in the back	opposite to
Result	and so	then	accordingly	in consequence
	so		as a result	therefore
			consequently	thereupon
			hence	thus

↻ Guideline 9.5

If more than one paragraph is based on the same reference, use wording that makes it clear.[5]

You may find yourself writing more than one paragraph based on a single reference. Provide the reference in the first paragraph, and provide transitions in subsequent paragraphs to make the continuity of the citation clear. Otherwise, readers might think that the ideas in subsequent paragraphs are yours. Example 9.5.1 shows how the identification of the source of the second two paragraphs is made clear. Note the terms in bold italics.

Example 9.5.1

Three paragraphs based on the same reference:

In one of the most comprehensive studies of consumer behavior during national recessions, Smith (2002) surveyed more than 1,000 consumers who....

In addition, the results *of the same survey* shed light on three related issues important to understanding....

Perhaps the most important result *of Smith's survey* was the segmentation of consumers into groups according to....

↻ Guideline 9.6

Avoid beginning your literature review with truisms.

Starting your literature review with a general "truism" (something all educated people probably know and believe) is usually a mistake. Instead, start with a paragraph that is specific to your review and contains specific information.

Example 9.6.1 shows a poor first paragraph followed by an improved first paragraph of a literature review. Note that the topic being reviewed is a particular nutritional labeling law. The second paragraph is superior because it gets straight to the point and names the law and its effects that will be covered in the literature review.

---

[5] This guideline is implied in Guideline 5.3. It also should be considered during the revision process.

Example 9.6.1

Poor first paragraph that states only truisms:

The importance of good nutrition is very widely recognized. One of the underlying requirements for making good nutritional decisions is having available reliable information on the nutritional contents of various foods and food products. Without such information, consumers will have a difficult time making decisions that are beneficial to their health.

Improved first paragraph, which refers directly to the topic of the review:

The 1990 Nutrition Labeling and Education Act (NLEA) dramatically changed nutrition labels on packaged foods in supermarkets, thereby increasing the amount of nutrition information available at the point of purchase. This law requires packaged foods to display nutrition information prominently in a new label format, namely, the Nutrition Facts panel. It also regulates serving size....[6]

↳ Guideline 9.7

Consider using a first paragraph that provides historical context—if the context is clearly on-target and interesting.

Interesting historical notes can be an effective way to begin a literature review. However, be careful that they relate directly to the topic of your review.

Example 9.7.1 is the first paragraph in a literature review on an *international* comparison of students' attitudes toward cheating. The historical anecdote is both interesting and relevant to the review.

Example 9.7.1

First paragraph that begins with an interesting historical anecdote:

The Chinese have been concerned about cheating for longer than most civilizations have been in existence. Over 2,000 years ago, prospective Chinese civil servants were given entrance exams in individual cubicles to prevent cheating and were searched as they entered the cubicles for crib notes. The penalty for being caught at cheating in ancient China was not a failing grade or expulsion, but death, which was applicable to both the examinees and the examiners (Brickman, 1961). Today, while we do not

---

[6] Balasubramanian & Cole (2002, p. 112).

execute students and their professors when cheating is discovered, it appears that we....[7]

♈ Guideline 9.8

Remove any material that is meant to be clever or amusing.

Scientific writing is serious writing. Therefore, it is inappropriate to attempt to entertain or to show how clever you can be in your use of language.

♈ Guideline 9.9

Revise to reduce the amount of anecdotal material.

An anecdote is a brief description of an interesting (or amusing) incident. Anecdotal evidence, which is based on isolated and perhaps nonrepresentative incidents, is one of the weakest forms of scientific evidence, hence it should be used very sparingly. Another drawback is that an incident that you find interesting or amusing may not be perceived as such by your readers.

♈ Guideline 9.10

When using the Harvard method for citation, it is often better to emphasize content over authorship.

In the Harvard method, citations to literature are provided by citing the surname(s) of the author(s) of a piece of literature followed by the year of publication. The reference list at the end of the literature review is arranged alphabetically by surnames when this method is used.[8]

Surnames of authors can be integrated into the sentences or placed in parentheses at the end of the sentences or paragraphs. Notice in Example 9.10.1 that the first version emphasizes authorship by referring to the authors

---

[7] Lupton & Chapman (2002, pp. 17–18).
[8] The Harvard method is also known as the APA method because it is recommended in the *Publication Manual of the American Psychological Association.*

first; the second one emphasizes content by putting the surnames of authors in parentheses at the end of the first sentence.

Example 9.10.1

Paragraph emphasizing authorship (usually not appropriate):

Mead (1955); Portes & Rumbaut (2001); and Sapocznik, Scopetta, Kurtines, & Arandale (1978) noted that when a family immigrates to a new country, the acculturation process typically is not uniform across generations of the family. When children learn the new culture more quickly than their parents, parental authority can be undermined....

Improved paragraph, which emphasizes content:

When a family immigrates to a new country, the acculturation process typically is not uniform across generations of the family (Mead, 1955; Portes & Rumbaut, 2001; Sapocznik, Scopetta, Kurtines, & Arandale, 1978). When children learn the new culture more quickly than their parents, parental authority can be undermined....[9]

The main exception to this guideline is when the authorship is important, such as when you refer to the developer of an important theory or when you are citing a study that is important because many others have cited and commented on it. Under these circumstances, authorship is important. Example 9.10.2 illustrates this.

Example 9.10.2

Paragraph emphasizing authorship by making the author's surname part of the sentence (appropriate in this circumstance because the author is someone who is often referenced):

Research on note taking and note review often references Wittrock's (1990) theory of generative processing. The supposition is that students who make associations between materials presented...and their own previous knowledge learn new material better than those students who do not generate links in the material....[10]

Another exception to this guideline occurs when you want to discuss differences of opinion between two or more researchers or theorists. Sometimes the text flows more smoothly if you use their names nonparenthetically, as was done in Example 9.10.3.

---

[9] Unger et. al (2002, p. 226).
[10] Elliot, Foster, & Stinson (2002, p. 26).

Example 9.10.3

Paragraph emphasizing authorship (may be appropriate when discussing differences of opinion among authors):

However, to date there is little empirical support for Langly's (2002) theory. What support exists is based on a logical analysis of....

In contrast, Doe's (2002) theory of XYZ has been investigated repeatedly for more than a decade. His theory supports the notion that....

↳ Guideline 9.11

Cross-check the references cited in the body of your review against those in your reference list at the end.

Make sure that the reference list at the end is complete and accurate. Attention to this matter can save you the embarrassment of having your readers call to your attention any missing or incorrect references in your paper. Note that the reference list serves the important purpose of helping your readers locate the original literature that you have cited.

The following types of errors are sometimes found in published journal articles: (a) the spelling of a surname in the citation is different from the spelling in the reference list, (b) the year given in the citation is different from the one in the reference list, and (c) a name in a citation does not appear in the reference list or vice versa.

↳ Guideline 9.12

Have your first draft critiqued by others. Pay careful attention to their criticisms and begin with the assumption that they are correct if they give you negative feedback.

A truism widely accepted in publishing is that "you can never have too many eyes look over a manuscript prior to publication." Your first concern should be to identify unclear material. Ask your reviewers to mark anything that is unclear to them with red ink and then discuss with them the marked sections. Avoid the pitfall of blaming your reviewers for not understanding your writing. If an educated person is confused by some sections of your first draft, be open to revising those sections. Otherwise, you might fall prey to the "clear if already known fallacy." Box 9C shows an analogy often used by one of the leading early researchers on the comprehensibility of written text. The analogy is designed to illustrate clearly that if you already know the material you are writing about, your expression of it may be clear to you but not to others.

Box 9C *An analogy that illustrates the "clear if already known fallacy."*[11]

> A tourist drove into town and was having trouble locating a motel at which he had a reservation. He stopped at a gas station to ask for directions. Trying to be helpful, the attendant said, "Go down this road and turn right where the old oak tree used to be before it died and was cut down. Then, turn left at the house that used to be painted red but now is some other color. Proceed for about a mile and the motel will be on your left."

Your second concern should be to identify mechanical errors in spelling, punctuation, and so on. You can sometimes get help with these matters at writing centers on college campuses. Note that even the most astute and well-trained proofreader will sometimes overlook an error here or there. Hence, do not rely on just one person to review your work for this purpose. Even if your literature review is for a class in which your instructor will not be deducting points (or lowering grades) for mechanical errors, it is difficult not to wonder if a student who is careless in these matters might not be careless in matters of content—causing instructors to scrutinize mechanically flawed papers more carefully. In addition, as a matter of pride, you will want to look your best for your readers by being as careful as possible regarding the mechanics of writing.

Concluding Comments

The guidelines in this chapter and the previous one apply to both qualitatively oriented and quantitatively oriented literature reviews. Both

---

[11] Loosely based on a personal communication with Edgar Dale, 1977.

types need strong, clearly written narratives to introduce the topics, establish their importance, and provide readers with an overview of the literature. The two approaches diverge when creating a synthesis on which to base conclusions. In a quantitatively oriented review, there will be much more emphasis on a statistical synthesis. In the next chapter, we will consider methods for balancing qualitative and quantitative approaches.

Exercise for Chapter 9

1. According to this chapter, why should you be generous in your use of headings and subheadings in your literature review?

2. If you have written your first draft, how many major headings and how many subheadings do you have? If you have not written it yet, list some of the headings and subheadings you might use.

3. According to this chapter, the "simplest model" for writing a paragraph is acceptable for use in literature reviews. Very briefly describe this model.

4. How is the term "rhetorical question" defined in this chapter? Is the use of rhetorical questions in literature reviews recommended in this chapter?

5. This statement appears in Box 9A: "Less experienced writers tend to supply too few transitions." Reflect on your first draft. Do you think you have used a sufficient number of transitional terms? Has the material in Box 9B helped you in the selection of transitional terms? Explain.

6. What should you make clear if more than one paragraph is based on a single reference?

7. Examine the first paragraph of your first draft of your literature review. Does it begin with a truism? If so, do you plan to change it? If not, does

your first paragraph provide information that is highly specific to your topic? Explain.

8. What is characterized in this chapter as "one of the weakest forms of scientific evidence"?

9. When using the Harvard method for citing references, what should you do if you want to emphasize content over authorship?

10. Have you obtained feedback on your first draft from others? If so, who critiqued it? Describe the types of changes, if any, that you made on the basis of their criticism. If you have not yet obtained feedback, whom do you plan to ask to review your first draft?

Chapter 10

Blending Qualitative and Quantitative Approaches

The purpose of this chapter is to provide guidelines on how to make a *qualitative* review more *quantitative* through the judicious reporting of statistical material in the review from the literature being covered—thus, arriving at a blend of approaches for writing literature reviews. The more statistical material you include in your qualitative review, the more quantitative it becomes. Hence, you should think of the two types as existing on a continuum from highly qualitative to highly quantitative. Four of the many points along this continuum are shown in Box 10A.

Box 10A *Four points on the continuum from highly qualitative to highly quantitative literature reviews.*

Almost exclusively qualitative	A blend leaning toward the qualitative	A blend leaning toward the quantitative	Very highly quantitative (i.e., a meta-analysis)
Absence of statistics. However, when reviewing statistical literature, statements that imply the use of statistics are made. Example: "Overall, the literature indicates that men generally have more XYZ than women."	Occasional mention of statistics by making statements such as: "Twelve of the 17 studies showed men had significantly more XYZ than women."	Frequent reporting of selected statistics such as: "Table 1 shows the percentages of men and women separately for each of the 17 studies on gender differences in XYZ."	Large numbers of statistics reported (often in extensive tables). Statistics are combined across studies. Example: "The average man in the 17 studies combined is 0.52 standard deviations above the average woman, which is a large effect size...."

ꙮ Guideline 10.1

Consider your audience's needs for reporting specific statistics in your literature review.

Your instructor may provide you with some guidance on this if he or she is your primary audience. For some audiences, such as those who have not studied statistics, you might want to write a highly qualitatively oriented literature review. For a committee of professors overseeing your work (e.g., doctoral dissertation), you might include much more quantification.

✍ Guideline 10.2

If you fail to state that a difference or relationship is statistically significant, your readers will assume that it is, which is acceptable if this is true.

Literature reviews typically contain many statements about differences and relationships reported in the literature. If reviewers were required to use the term "statistically significant" each time they mentioned a difference, many literature reviews would be cluttered with this term, which might appear dozens of times in a review.

Statements such as the one in Example 10.2.1 are extremely common in literature reviews. Notice that the statement does *not* indicate that the benefits for those who exercise regularly are significantly greater than for those who do not. However, it is safe to assume that they are; otherwise, the reviewer would warn us with some type of caution such as "preliminary research has revealed an *in*significant increase in physical benefits from regular exercise."

Example 10.2.1

A statement about differences without mentioning statistical significance (acceptable if the differences are significant):

Regular physical activity has physical (e.g., improving cardiovascular endurance) and psychological (e.g., increasing self-esteem) benefits for children and adolescents (United States Department of Health and Human Services [USDHHS], 1996, 2000)....[1]

---

[1] Hausenblas, Nigg, Downs, Fleming, & Connaughton (2002, p. 436).

Of course, there will be times when you will want to report on *insignificant* differences. This is especially true when comparing a difference between groups. Consider Example 10.2.2. Readers will assume that the first difference is statistically significant and assume that the second one is not because it is referred to as "no difference."

Example 10.2.2

A statement about differences with the first part implying statistical significance and the second part implying insignificance:

While young adult Republicans differed from young adult Democrats on the XYZ issue, there was no difference between middle-aged Republicans and middle-aged Democrats on this issue.

Note that the term "no difference" as used in Example 10.2.2 almost always means "no statistically significant difference." When we compare two large samples (such as large samples of middle-aged Republicans and Democrats), it is almost certain that some difference will be observed even if it is as small as 62.5% for Republicans and 62.3% for Democrats. If this difference is not statistically significant, reviewers typically use "no difference" as shorthand for "no statistically significant difference." This is an accepted practice when writing literature reviews.

✥ Guideline 10.3

Consider pointing out especially large (or strong) and especially small (or weak) differences or relationships.

As you know from Guideline 7.10, just because a difference (or relationship) is statistically significant does *not* necessarily mean that it is large (or strong). It means only that it is *reliable*. Even very small differences can be quite reliable (i.e., statistically significant). An example that illustrates this is given in the discussion of Guideline 7.10. Because this is such an important point, consider the following additional example: A third-grade teacher very precisely measures the heights of the students in his class on the first Monday of September and on the first Monday of October each year and records the data. After 35 years, he carefully examines the data and sees that year after year, there is a minuscule increase in height from September to October. Thus, he has detected a *reliable but small difference*. A statistical significance test tells us *only* whether a difference (or relationship) is *reliable*, which it would be in this example if measurements were taken across a large enough number of years. It does *not* address the issue of whether the difference is large.

One of the most common flaws in writing literature reviews is to treat all statistically significant differences or relationships as being equal in magnitude. Thus, it is common to see discussions of literature as shown in Example 10.3.1. This problem has been fixed in Example 10.3.2. Notice that the "fix" does not require reference to any specific statistics.

Example 10.3.1

A discussion of relationships in which all are treated as equal due to the lack of differentiation in terms of magnitude (not recommended):

One of the most consistent findings in research on achievement testing is that there is a positive relationship between scores on vocabulary knowledge tests and scores on reading comprehension tests. Positive relationships have also consistently been found between scores on reading comprehension tests and scores on mathematics word problem tests.

Example 10.3.2

An improved version of Example 10.3.1 (differences from Example 10.3.1 are shown in italics):

One of the most consistent findings in research on achievement testing is that there is a *strong* positive relationship between scores on vocabulary knowledge tests and scores on reading comprehension tests. *Although* positive relationships have also consistently been found between scores on reading comprehension tests and scores on mathematics word problem tests, *these relationships are almost always much weaker than the relationships between vocabulary and reading comprehension.*

Box 10B *One of the most common flaws (see Guidelines 7.10 and 10.3).*

> One of the most common flaws in writing literature reviews is to treat all statistically significant differences or relationships as being equal in magnitude.

↳ Guideline 10.4

Examine your literature review to identify vague terms that refer to quantities, and consider replacing them with specific statistics.

Terms such as "more," "less," "stronger," "weaker," "higher," "lower," "majority," and "minority" refer to quantities. If the quantities you have referred to with these terms are simple and easy to understand, consider supplementing them with the specific statistics. The specificity of the second sentence in Example 10.4.1 makes it superior to the first.

Example 10.4.1

Two statements based on the same piece of literature. The second one names specific statistics (as they appeared in the original source):

First statement: Although a minority of AFDC [Aid to Families with Dependent Children] recipients are married women (Moffitt, Reville, & Walker, 1998)....

Second statement: Although 19 percent to 30 percent of AFDC recipients are married women (Moffitt, Reville, & Walker, 1998)....[2]

↳ Guideline 10.5

Consider summarizing key statistics in a table.

Readers may find it easier to peruse and get an overview of the statistics on a topic if they are tabled. If you table values, you can point out the highlights of the table without necessarily repeating the exact statistics in your narrative. Example 10.5.1 shows a portion of a table containing specific statistics that were included in a literature review.

Note that when statistics on an issue are scattered throughout the narrative of a literature review, it can be difficult for readers to make comparisons across studies. Notice that the table in Example 10.5.1 makes it easy to compare percentages across studies as well as to identify those that do not report percentages.

---

[2] Cheng, T. (2002, p. 161).

Example 10.5.1

Table containing statistics that appeared in a literature review of research on needlestick injuries among healthcare workers. (For instructional purposes, only two of the seven columns and only five of the 16 study findings are shown here):[3]

Study	Study Findings
Ribner (1990)	Decreased injury due to recapping from 61% to 16% of total needlesticks.
Haiduven (1992)	Decreased injuries by 45%; decreased injury due to recapping by 53%.
Orenstein (1995)	Decrease in injuries from 33 to 14; cost of each prevented needlestick estimated at $789.
CDC (1997b)	46% of injuries unreported; 20% of safety units not activated.
Lawrence (1997)	Decreased IV injury rate; 94% user satisfaction reported.

⤷ Guideline 10.6

Avoid overburdening readers with statistics in the narrative of your review.

Most of you will have collected at least several research reports that contain many statistics. In writing your literature review, you should provide an overview, including your evaluation of research studies and other literature, followed by a synthesis and conclusions. If you incorporate too many statistics in the narrative portion of your review, you are likely to burden your readers with too much specific information. Since most of the studies you will refer to are already published, readers can consult the studies for additional statistics if needed.

This guideline can be implemented in four ways. First, it can be done through the judicious selection of statistics to state in your review. For instance, a report that you are citing may have many means[4] and standard deviations. Depending on the point(s) you are making, you might mention, for example, only the highest and lowest means in the entire set of studies

---

[3] Porta, Handelman, & McGovern (1999, p. 240).
[4] The arithmetic mean is the most widely used average in research.

(and omit all the standard deviations), as illustrated in Example 10.6.1. Of course, if the topic of your paper is "risk-taking among juvenile delinquents," you might want to discuss the findings in greater detail. On the other hand, if your topic is "how to measure risk-taking propensity" (in general), the studies in Example 10.6.1 might be only a minor subset of the literature you have collected, and the amount of detail in Example 10.6.1 might be sufficient.

Example 10.6.1

A statement citing only two means, which show the range of results across a large number of means found in a large number of studies:

Means on the Avis Risk-Taking Scale in the 23 studies in which it has been used in published research range from 39.36 in a study of juvenile delinquents (Doe, 2003) to 18.97 in a study of high school honor students (Smith, 2001). A score of 39.36 is far above the clinical cutting point for abnormally high risk-taking propensities while a score of 18.97 is near the national average of 21.95.

Note that when reporting a range of values that vary greatly, such as we see in Example 10.6.1, it is desirable to point out any distinctive characteristics of the group with the highest value (in this case, being juvenile delinquents is distinctive) as well as distinctive characteristics of the group with the lowest value (in this case, high school honor students). Also, if you know how the "average" person performs, such as the national average on a published test or scale, it is helpful to include it as a reference point for readers of your review.

A second way to implement Guideline 10.6 is to cite specific statistics for only a limited number of studies that are especially important in helping you create your synthesis and arrive at conclusions. For the other studies you cite, you might report on differences and relationships in words without statistics (while mentioning which ones are large or strong and which ones are small or weak).

Third, you can use tables, as suggested in Guideline 10.5, which your readers can refer to for specific statistics when they want to do so while you point out only the statistical highlights in your narrative.

Fourth, you can include a brief meta-analysis within a qualitative review, a possibility that is discussed in the next chapter.

✍ Guideline 10.7

If a particular statistic is especially important in helping you to create a synthesis, consider commenting on the quality of the study that generated the statistic.

This guideline was alluded to in the previous one. However, it is important enough to be discussed as a separate guideline. As you know from Guideline 8.13, you should consider commenting on the quality of the research you cite in your literature review. Often, this can be done with phrases that indicate the quality of the research. Box 10C shows some phrases that can be used to indicate that a study is weak or strong. If you do not use any phrases of these types when citing studies, readers will probably assume that you believe that they are reasonable in quality.

Relying on and citing statistics from methodologically weak studies to support the main thrust of the synthesis you provide in your literature review is potentially misleading unless you point out those weaknesses. You can point them out by discussing the methodology of such key studies in some detail or, at least, by using one or more of the phrases of the type shown in the first column of Box 10C. It is usually undesirable to provide detailed evaluations of all studies that you cite. The more important a study (and its resulting statistics) is to your conclusions, the more detailed your evaluation should be.

Box 10C *Phrases that indicate strengths and weaknesses. (Consider using them when discussing statistical results.)*

Phrases that indicate weaknesses:	Phrases that indicate strengths:
In a preliminary study, Doe (2002) reported data that indicates....	A definitive study by Doe (2002) indicates....
The results of a local survey by Doe (2002) suggest....	A major nationwide poll conducted by Doe (2002) supports....
	Continued →

Box 10C *Continued*

Phrases that indicate weaknesses:	Phrases that indicate strengths:
While the results of Doe's (2002) pilot study are interesting, additional research should be conducted in order to confirm the major findings that….	While the earlier studies on the topic had mixed results, Doe's (2002) study is probably the most reliable because she used random….
All five studies on the effects of XYZ have two major flaws: use of volunteer samples and lack of random assignment to….	The use of random assignment in the five studies on the effects of XYZ give us confidence in the finding that XYZ has an important effect on….

It is important to note that it is quite acceptable to rely heavily on methodologically weak studies in creating a synthesis and reaching conclusions in a literature review if they provide the best available evidence. Of course, you will want to point out the weaknesses of the studies in your narrative and warn your readers that your synthesis and conclusions are tentative because they are based on weak studies.

ᔐ Guideline 10.8

Consider using wording that indicates which statements are based on statistical information and which are not.

Sometimes literature reviews are flawed because readers cannot determine from the wording which statements are data-based (with statistics) and which are not data-based. Example 10.8.1 shows two statements from a single literature review, both of which are clearly data-based. The data-based nature of the first one is clear from the mention of a specific statistic (20.5%). The second one is clearly data-based because of the use of the terms "studies" and "study." Other phrases and terms that are cues that the assertions are data-based are: "In an experiment….," "This survey shows….," "Smith (2003) investigated the relationship between….," and "Researchers have found that…."

Example 10.8.1

Two statements from a literature review that are clearly data-based:

First statement: Child poverty is currently 20.5% (CDF, 1998)....

Second statement: Studies have shown mixed results in understanding the impact of homelessness beyond poverty. A study by Bassuk and Rosenberg (1988) suggests....[5]

Reviewers also use terms and phrases to indicate that a statement is *not* data-based. Two samples are shown in Example 10.8.2. The term "speculated" in the first statement and the term "mentioned the possibility" in the second one suggest that the assertions are not based on data. Other terms and phrases that indicate the lack of underlying data are: "Doe (2003) argued that....," "It is reasonable to infer from everyday observations that....," "On the basis of anecdotal evidence, it seems reasonable to conclude that....," and "Jackson (2002) suggested that...."

Example 10.8.2

Two statements that are clearly not data-based:

First statement: Doe (2003) has speculated that consumer confidence in the economy will rise....

Second statement: Several authors have mentioned the possibility that consumer confidence in the economy rises when....

Failure to indicate whether statistics underlie a statement in a literature review is a flaw because the distinction between an "opinion" and a "statistical finding" is important to many readers. Example 10.8.3 shows statements that are not clear in terms of this issue because there are no cues of the types shown in Examples 10.8.1 and 10.8.2.

Example 10.8.3

Two statements from literature reviews that are unclear as to whether they are data-based (not recommended):

First statement: While the impact of homelessness cannot be separated from poverty, sustained homelessness during childhood is a life event that

---

[5] Schmitz, Wagner, & Menke (2001, p. 69).

has a tremendous impact throughout a child's adult life (Smith, 2003). [*Note*: It is not clear from this statement whether Smith provides statistics on the "impact of homelessness."]

Second statement: Teachers know the importance of early reading comprehension achievement to later success in school (Jones, 2002). [*Note*: It is not clear from this statement whether Jones provides statistics on the teachers' knowledge.]

☙ Guideline 10.9
Consider discussing the statistical support, if any, for important theories that you describe in your literature review.

The importance of considering and discussing theories in your literature review has been stressed throughout this book. Theories help us to conceptually tie together a number of diverse variables. As a result, they enable us to make predictions. The ultimate test of a theory is whether empirical results confirm the predictions made on the basis of the theory. Thus, even if you are disinclined to discuss research methods and statistical results in other parts of your literature review, you should consider doing so when discussing theories that are important in helping you arrive at a synthesis on which you base the conclusions of your literature review.

Concluding Comments

The extent to which you quantify your literature review by citing statistical results is a matter of judgment. You should consider the needs of your audience and your purpose (provide a broad general overview versus a detailed discussion of findings reported in the literature). Many of you might want to strive for a balance to avoid the possible criticisms that either (a) your review is too broad and general and, hence, you have failed to fully support your conclusions or (b) your review is so riddled with a multitude of statistics that readers find it difficult to obtain a good overview from your literature review. You can avoid both of these criticisms through the judicious selection of statistics to include in your review and by following the other guidelines in this chapter.

In the next chapter, we will consider a highly mathematical method for arriving at a synthesis of research literature called a "meta-analysis." Even though the method for ultimately arriving at a synthesis is purely mathematical, a report on a meta-analysis contains many of the same elements as a qualitative review. Also, you can consider incorporating a "mini" meta-analysis within a larger qualitative review, a possibility that will be discussed in the next chapter.

Exercise for Chapter 10

1. According to this chapter, is it necessary to choose between a dichotomy of "highly qualitative approach" versus "highly quantitative approach" when writing a literature review? Explain.

2. Suppose that a reviewer made a statement such as this in her literature review: "The mean for women was higher than the mean for men (Doe, 2003)." According to this chapter, what are readers likely to assume about the statistical significance of the difference between the two means?

3. Very briefly explain why you should consider pointing out the size of differences even if they are statistically significant. In other words, is it sufficient to say that a difference is statistically significant without mentioning its size? Explain.

4. In this chapter, what is named as being "one of the most common flaws in writing literature reviews"?

5. At this point, to what extent do you plan to quantify your literature review? Do you plan to use a table to report key statistics? Explain.

6. According to this chapter, is it possible to "over quantify" a literature review? Explain.

7. According to this chapter, is it acceptable to rely heavily on methodologically weak studies (and their statistics) in creating a synthesis and reaching conclusions in a literature review? If yes, what should you point out to your readers if you do this?

8. Write two terms or phrases that would help tip off your readers that a statement you are citing from the literature is data-based?

9. Is it appropriate to discuss statistics when discussing theories? Explain.

10. If you have already written your literature review, read it again to determine if there are points at which the addition of some specific statistical information would strengthen your review. If you find any, describe at least one and come to class prepared to discuss it.

11. In addition to the possibility of incorporating some statistics in your literature review, are there other suggestions in this chapter that you plan to use in revising the draft of your literature review? If yes, name one and come to class prepared to discuss it.

Chapter 11

Preparing a Meta-Analysis

The prefix "meta-" means "more comprehensive; transcending others." A meta-analysis is a statistical analysis that transcends others by mathematically combining the results of various studies conducted by different researchers to obtain an overall result (a mathematical synthesis).

While an entire book could be written about meta-analysis, in this chapter we will cover only certain fundamentals that will allow you to perform basic meta-analyses. Although they may be "basic," they can make an important contribution to advancing knowledge on a topic.

Let us move quickly from the abstract to the specific by considering how percentages might be treated and discussed in a meta-analysis.

⅄ Guideline 11.1

A meta-analysis of results presented as percentages in various studies can be conducted by calculating a weighted average of the percentages.

The raw statistics from three national polls (conducted by three different researchers) on public attitudes toward the XYZ issue are presented in Box 11A. In each case, the pollster has reported the number of people surveyed and the percentage who said "yes" when asked a question about the issue. Let us assume that the three researchers used approximately the same wording in the question on the issue. As you can see, they obtained three different percentages. Such differences are to be expected because of sampling error (each pollster used only a small sample of the entire national population). Based on these three *samples*, what is our best estimate of the *true* percentage of the *population* that would answer "yes" if everyone in the population were polled?

Box 11A *Results of three national polls on the XYZ issue.*

Poll 1	Poll 2	Poll 3
Number of people interviewed: 595	Number of people interviewed: 1,028	Number of people interviewed: 1,440
Percentage who answered "yes": 72%	Percentage who answered "yes": 51%	Percentage who answered "yes": 50%

To answer the question, you might be tempted simply to sum the percentages (72% + 51% + 50% = 173%) and divide the sum by the number of polls (173%/3 = 57.66%, which rounds to 58%). However, notice that Polls 2 and 3 had many more respondents than Poll 1. Hence, their results are probably more reliable and should be given more weight in determining the combined average percentage across the three studies. The first steps in getting the weighted average are shown in Box 11B.

Box 11B *First steps in calculating a weighted percentage.*

Column 1	Column 2	Column 3	Column 4
	Total number of respondents.	Percentage who said "yes."	Calculate the number who said "yes" by multiplying.
Poll 1	595	72%	(595)(0.72) = 428
Poll 2	1,028	51%	(1,028)(0.51) = 524
Poll 3	1,440	50%	(1,440)(0.50) = 720
Sum of Column 2 = 3,063		**Sum of Column 3 = 1,672**	

From Box 11B, we now know that across all three studies combined, there were 3,063 respondents of which 1,672 said "yes." Using these two figures, we can calculate the percentage in the usual way (dividing the *part* [1,672] by the *whole* [3,063] and multiplying by 100%). Performing this arithmetic, we get 1,672/3,063 = 0.5458 x 100% = 54.58%, which rounds to 55%, which is the weighted average percentage across the three studies. The result of this meta-analysis could be described in a literature review with a statement such as the one in Example 11.1.1.

Example 11.1.1

Sample statement of results of the meta-analysis of percentages:[1]

Three national polls were conducted on public attitudes toward XYZ. The results of the three polls are shown in Table 1 below. Note that the percentages that responded "yes" vary from 50% in the poll with the largest sample (Smith, 2003) to 72% in the poll with the smallest sample size (Doe, 2003). The average percentage that has been weighted to take account of differences in sample size in the three polls is 55%, which indicates that a majority of the population is in favor of XYZ. This percentage is based on a total sample of 3,063 respondents.

Table 1

Percentage Who Answered "Yes" on XYZ

	Doe (2003)	Jones (2003)	Smith (2003)
Percentage	72%	51%	50%
(*n*)	(595)	(1,028)	(1,440)

As you will see from the guidelines in the rest of this chapter and by examining Model Literature Review 3, a meta-analysis involves much more than merely stating the statistical results of individual studies and then providing a weighted average of them. Nevertheless, you have now seen an example of the basic technique for obtaining a mathematical synthesis: obtaining a weighted average of the results across various studies on the same issue.

Note that a *major advantage* of meta-analysis is that it provides an average result that is based on a larger sample than was used in any of the individual studies on which it is based. In this case, our best estimate of 55% is based on the answers of 3,063 respondents, which is twice as large as the answer of 50% from the single poll with the largest sample (Poll 3, which had 1,440 respondents). For reasons that are typically covered in statistics

---

[1] Calculating the standard error (margin of error) for a percentage and testing to determine whether the weighted average of 55% is significantly higher than 50% are topics covered in introductory statistics books. These topics are beyond the scope of the present chapter, which is designed to show you how to calculate basic statistics for a meta-analysis, a topic seldom covered in introductory statistics textbooks.

and research methods books, national polls usually are based on about 1,500 respondents *or* less. Thus, 3,063 is a very large sample for a national poll.

Box 11C *A major advantage of meta-analysis.*

> A major advantage of meta-analysis is that the combined answer is based on the combined sample, which is larger than the sample in any one of the underlying studies.

Box 11D shows examples of how the results of the three polls might be handled by writers of literature reviews with three different orientations: highly qualitative, with no mention of specific statistics; moderately quantitative, with some mention of specific statistics; and highly quantitative (a meta-analysis). The statement in the third column of Box 11D is analogous to the statement of results in Example 11.1.1.

Box 11D *Examples of qualitative and quantitative statements.*

Highly qualitative (no mention of specific statistics)	Moderately quantitative (some statistics reported)	Highly quantitative (meta-analysis stating combined results)
In the three national polls on the XYZ issue, a majority answered "yes," indicating that a majority of the population is in favor of it.	In the three national polls on the XYZ issue, between 50% and 72% answered "yes," indicating that a majority of the population is in favor of it. OR Fifty percent, 51%, and 72% of the respondents in the three national polls on the "XYZ" issue answered "yes," indicating....	The number of respondents and the percentages who answered "yes" in the three national polls are shown in Table 1. While there is wide variation, the best estimate based on a weighted average of the three results is that 55% of the population is in favor of it.

Note: If there were a large number of polls, a reviewer who mentioned only the range (e.g., 50% to 72%) would provide much less quantification than one who presented all the percentages in a table and discussed the highlights of the table (moderately quantified). However, presenting all the raw statistics as well as a mathematical combination (a meta-analysis) provides the most highly quantified synthesis of the literature.

✍ Guideline 11.2

The beginning of a meta-analysis should be similar to the beginning of a qualitative review.

Regardless of your approach (highly qualitative through highly quantitative), you should begin by establishing the importance of the topic, provide an overview of the types of literature available (the scope of the literature), and comment on its quality based on your evaluations of it. You should also indicate how various theories relate to your topic whenever possible. Example 11.2.1 shows the beginning of a meta-analysis journal article. Notice that it could also be the beginning of a highly qualitative literature review because the author is introducing the topic and providing some background on it, which should be done at the beginning of any type of literature review.

Example 11.2.1

The beginning of a meta-analysis review. A beginning that could also be the beginning of a qualitatively oriented literature review:

Psychologists have long debated whether emotions are universal versus whether they vary by culture. These issues have been extensively summarized elsewhere, and we do not reiterate them (e.g., Ekman, 1972, 1994; Izard, 1971; Mesquita & Frijda, 1992; Mesquita, Frijda, & Scherer, 1997; Russell, 1994; Scherer & Wallbott, 1994). Although many theorists have taken extreme positions and provoked lively debate, recent theoretical models have attempted to account for both universality and cultural variation by specifying which particular aspects of emotion show similarities and differences across cultural boundaries....[2]

✍ Guideline 11.3

When writing a meta-analysis, indicate the search terms you used as well as the databases that you searched.

Traditionally, those who conduct meta-analyses describe in great detail how they searched the literature for relevant publications—indicating which databases they searched, whether they searched for unpublished studies such as doctoral dissertations and convention reports, and what terms they used (such as "anxiety" and variations on it such as "anxious"). Although this

---

[2] Elfenbein & Ambady (2002, p. 203).

tradition is closely associated with meta-analysis, those who conduct qualitative reviews should consider adopting this tradition because including this information in a literature review reassures readers that a thorough search has been conducted (or alternatively, readers will see that an important term or database was overlooked in the search). In either case, readers will be better informed if they are given this information.

The description of the search for literature for a meta-analysis is usually quite detailed, as the excerpt in Example 11.3.1 illustrates.

Example 11.3.1

Portions of a description of the search for literature for a meta-analysis:

We used several procedures to ensure that we had included existing studies. First, we searched several electronic indexes using the keyword *trust*: PsycINFO (1967–2000), SocioFile (1974–2000), ABI/Inform (1985–2000), and *Dissertation Abstracts* (1861–1999). The search identified over 15,500 studies that were reviewed for consideration.... Second, we examined the reference sections of books and articles that provided a narrative review of the trust literature (e.g., Dirks & Ferrin, 2001...). Third, we manually searched for studies in the following [eleven] journals from 1980 to the present: *Academy of Management Journal, Administrative Science Quarterly*.... Fourth, we gathered unpublished research by contacting approximately 90 researchers who were considered likely to have relevant data. Unpublished studies were included to minimize publication bias (Rosenthal, 1979).[3]

↳ Guideline 11.4

Consider discussing efforts made to overcome the "file drawer" effect (i.e., publication bias) on the outcome(s) of your meta-analysis.

Traditionally, those who conduct meta-analysis concern themselves with the "file drawer" effect, also known as a "publication bias," which is mentioned in the last sentence of Example 11.3.1. Both terms refer to the

---

[3] Dirks & Ferrin (2002, p. 617).

possibility that researchers who obtain statistically *insignificant* results may not submit them for publication (on the assumption that editors want to publish research that has statistically significant results). Thus, in effect, researchers with insignificant results may be stashing their data in a "never to be published" file drawer. Those who conduct meta-analyses typically mention the possibility of a publication bias (file drawer effect) and indicate whether they have searched for unpublished studies by examining theses and dissertations, contacting researchers who have been conducting research on the topic to see if they have filed away studies that had insignificant results, and so on. (Notice that in Example 11.3.1, the reviewers mention that they searched *Dissertation Abstracts* and contacted almost 90 researchers in an effort to overcome publication bias.)

To the extent that there is publication bias that has not been overcome when preparing the meta-analysis, the results will be inflated because the studies that are not published (and, thus, are not included in the meta-analysis) may tend to have smaller (or even negative) results that are statistically insignificant. In other words, the mathematical average will be higher than it should be if only studies with strong effects (which tend to be the studies that are published) are included when averaging.

Although a thorough search for unpublished research reports is traditional when conducting meta-analyses, those who write qualitative reviews should also consider being thorough and making efforts to uncover unpublished research reports. Whether qualitatively oriented or quantitatively oriented, a reviewer should report on these efforts, if any.

Box 11E *Two traditions followed by those who conduct meta-analyses that might be followed more often by those who write qualitative reviews.*

1. Describe in detail how you searched for related literature. See Guideline 11.3.

2. Consider whether there may be studies on your topic that are unpublished because the results were insignificant. Attempt to locate such studies and incorporate them in the review. See Guideline 11.4.

⅏ Guideline 11.5

Decide whether you will exclude methodologically weak studies from your meta-analysis.

A very weak study in terms of methodology could have a strong effect on the outcome of a meta-analysis if it has a large number of participants (or if it was one of only a small number of studies such as one study out of a total of three). While a qualitative reviewer can mention a very weak study and dismiss its importance because of its weaknesses, a very weak study in a meta-analysis counts as much as a very strong study that has the same number of participants.

While excluding weak studies from a meta-analysis is a matter of some controversy, it seems better to exclude them *if* they are excluded on the basis of pre-established, objective criteria such as "All studies without a control group will be excluded."

Some writers suggest that all studies, regardless of their weaknesses, should be included in a meta-analysis. Their rationale is that certain types of weaknesses in some studies might counterbalance other types of weaknesses in other studies when they are all averaged mathematically. The possibility of a "counterbalancing effect of weaknesses" seems most likely to happen when there are a relatively large number of studies. When there are only a small number, the results of the weakest study might overwhelm the results of the small number of strong studies when results are mathematically combined.

In your literature review, you should mention whether you omitted methodologically weak studies and, if so, what criteria were used to identify those that were omitted.

⅏ Guideline 11.6

If some studies are excluded from the meta-analysis for reasons other than weak methodology, provide specific reasons and/or criteria for their exclusion.

When studies on the topic were excluded from a meta-analysis, readers will want to know the basis for excluding them. By being specific about the reasons for exclusion, readers can be reassured that there was no bias (intentional or otherwise) in the final selection of studies on which the meta-analysis is based.

To illustrate this guideline, consider Example 11.6.1. The authors of the example conducted a meta-analysis of the effectiveness of computer-assisted instruction (CAI) in supporting the teaching of beginning reading. Of the several hundred publications they initially identified, only 42 survived the selection criteria that they describe in their review. Some of the criteria they used are shown in the example.

Example 11.6.1

Criteria used to exclude studies from a meta-analysis on the effectiveness of CAI in supporting the teaching of beginning reading:

The first round of selections was conducted by removing the references published before 1990 on the assumption that older studies were represented in available reviews.... A subsequent selection was carried out using abstracts. One selection criterion was that the publication should report an empirical study. Position papers and publications that contained only descriptions of CAI programs or suggestions for teachers were excluded. We also eliminated studies reporting on samples of students with severe or multiple disabilities such as aphasia, deafness, or blindness. We wanted to limit our focus to the population of modal or regular students....[4]

☙ Guideline 11.7

Consider including one or more moderator variables in your meta-analysis. If they are included, provide a rationale for their selection.

A "moderator" variable is one used to form separate groups for separate analyses. For instance, in a recently published meta-analysis of the literature

---

[4] Blok, Oostdam, Otter, & Overmatt (2002, pp. 107–108).

on the magnitude of genetic and environmental influences on antisocial behavior, the authors conducted meta-analyses in which they included a number of moderator variables, one of which was gender. They examined the magnitude of genetic and environmental influences in separate meta-analyses for men and women, compared the two results, and found no significant differences.[5]

The rationale for including each moderator variable should be stated in the report of the meta-analysis. For instance, because a much higher proportion of men than women are incarcerated in jails and prisons, the use of gender as a moderator variable seems justified in a meta-analysis on antisocial behavior. Example 11.7.1 shows the rationale for including undergraduate major (academic discipline) as a moderator variable in their meta-analysis of the validity of the Graduate Record Examination (GRE).

Example 11.7.1

Rationale for including type of undergraduate major (academic discipline) as a moderator variable in a meta-analysis of the validity of the GRE:

Several variables may moderate the relationship between scores on the GRE and performance in graduate school. First, the predictive validity of the GRE may vary by academic discipline. Although there are many similarities in some of the fundamental tasks required of all graduate students, there are differences in the type of training and demands of different academic areas. To investigate the impact of academic field on the predictive validity of the GRE tests, we conducted separate analyses for subsamples representing four broad disciplines: humanities, the social sciences, life sciences, and math–physical sciences.[6]

☙ Guideline 11.8

Because a meta-analysis typically can be conducted on only some of the literature on a topic, consider incorporating a meta-analysis within a larger qualitative review.

---

[5] Rhee & Waldman (2002, p. 490).
[6] Kuncel, Hezlett, & Ones (2001, p. 168).

Three types of literature cannot be incorporated into a meta-analysis. First, there is speculative literature, including some literature on new theories that have not been researched yet. These cannot be included because they do not contain statistics. Second, some research reports do not contain a sufficient number of statistics. For instance, when means are combined in meta-analyses, which we will consider below, standard deviations must be used. If a research report provides means without standard deviations, by default, it will be excluded. Third, some research reports contain statistics that are not compatible with the majority of the quantitative research that will be combined mathematically. For instance, most reports with averages will contain means, which can be easily combined mathematically. However, some reports will contain medians or modes (and no means) as averages, which will lead to the exclusion of these reports in a meta-analysis.[7]

One way around this exclusionary problem is to write a qualitative review that incorporates all relevant literature (perhaps even mentioning very weak studies that might be excluded from a meta-analysis; see Guideline 11.5) and combine it with a meta-analysis of the literature on the topic that lends itself to meta-analytic techniques.

✳ Guideline 11.9
Meta-analyses are often conducted by standardizing the difference between means using Cohen's *d*.

The mean, by far, is the most commonly reported average. It is obtained by adding a set of scores and dividing by the number of scores. Frequently, researchers use means to estimate the average difference between two groups such as the average difference in income between high school dropouts and high school graduates or the average difference between experimental and control groups in an experiment.

---

[7] Methods for calculating missing statistics from those that are reported, or for estimating them in various ways by making certain mathematical assumptions, are beyond the scope of this book.

Let us consider a concrete example that illustrates the need for calculating Cohen's *d* when comparing means. Suppose there have been 15 experiments on the effects of an antidepressant drug given to the experimental groups. In each study, the control group received a placebo. At the end of each study, the level of depression of the participants was assessed. *If all experimenters used the same instruments*, we could simply average the means (while first weighting each one according to the number of participants such as we did with percentages near the beginning of this chapter). Unfortunately, you will typically find wide variation in how a variable such as depression is measured. In one study, the participants might be rated on a scale from 1 to 10. In another study, a published self-report instrument designed to measure depression on a scale from 20 to 80 might be used. In yet another, a questionnaire developed by the researcher that yields scores from 200 to 800 might be used. By default, the mean in the first case must be between 1 and 10; in the second case, it must be between 20 and 80; and in the third, it must be between 200 and 800. For just these first three of the 15 studies, we might have results such as those shown in Box 11F.

Describing the information in Box 11F, a qualitative researcher could state that in all studies, the control group was found to have higher levels of depression than the experimental group. The reviewer could also indicate which, if any, of the differences were statistically significant, which experiment had the largest sample size, which one(s) seem to be stronger methodologically, and finally, arrive at a conclusion and synthesis regarding the results of the three experiments without using precise mathematical procedures, thus avoiding the problem caused by the varying score scales used by the three experimenters.

When considering how to calculate the weighted average of the means, however, an individual conducting a meta-analysis faces an important problem. Averaging the means will give undue weight to the third study because the scale measures depression on a scale from 200 to 800, which by default will yield much higher means than the other two studies that have scales from 1 to 10 and 20 to 80. Thus, an individual conducting a meta-analysis faces the major problem caused by different researchers using different scales to measure the same constructs (in this case, depression).

Box 11F *Means (m), standard deviations (s), and numbers of cases (n) for experimental and control groups in three experiments on the effects of the same antidepressant drug employing different measures of depression.*

	Experimental Group	Control Group
Study 1	$m = 6.27$ $s = 4.04$ $n = 15$	$m = 8.99$ $s = 5.99$ $n = 15$
Study 2	$m = 50.55$ $s = 31.76$ $n = 35$	$m = 61.26$ $s = 30.55$ $n = 40$
Study 3	$m = 525.33$ $s = 277.01$ $n = 110$	$m = 587.02$ $s = 301.33$ $n = 120$

The solution for this problem is to *standardize* the scales and express the differences between the control groups and the experimental groups on a standard scale such as Cohen's *d*, which is a measure of "effect size."[8] Doing this is mathematically quite easy. For those who have not taken statistics, the difficult part will be understanding *why* Cohen's *d* standardizes means that are initially expressed on different scales. Let us do the easy part first (the mathematics), which should help you understand *why* it standardizes them.

To compute Cohen's *d* for each study, simply subtract the control group mean from the experimental group mean and divide the difference by the standard deviation of the control group.[9] These calculations are shown in Box 11G, where the subscript "$_e$" in the formula for *d* stands for "experimental group" and "$_c$" stands for "control group."

---

[8] Some writers mistakenly use "effect size" as a synonym for Cohen's *d*. In fact, *d* is only one of a number of statistics that can be used to estimate effect size (i.e., the magnitude of a difference or relationship on a common scale). The other frequently used measure of effect size is the correlation coefficient, which we will consider later in this chapter.
[9] Some reviewers recommend using a special type of average of the two standard deviations as the divisor.

Box 11G *Calculation of Cohen's* d *for Study 1 using statistics in Box 11F.*
Values of Cohen's d *for other two studies are shown.*[10]

	Experimental Group	Control Group
Study 1 $d = -0.45$	$m = 6.27$ $s = 4.04$	$m = 8.99$ $s = 5.99$
Calculation of *d* for Study 1: $$d = \frac{m_e - m_c}{s_c} = \frac{6.27 - 8.99}{5.99} = \frac{-2.72}{5.99} = -0.45$$		
Study 2 $d = -0.35$	$m = 50.55$ $s = 31.76$	$m = 61.26$ $s = 30.55$
Study 3 $d = -0.20$	$m = 525.33$ $s = 277.01$	$m = 587.02$ $s = 301.33$

By calculating *d* for all three studies, we have *standardized* the expression of the amount (i.e., magnitude) of the differences between the three pairs of means. How did we do this? By dividing the differences between the means by the *standard deviation* associated with the control group. Having done this, we now know by *how many standard deviations* each experimental group's mean exceeds the control group's mean. For instance, for Study 1, *d* = –0.45, which means that the mean of the experimental group is 45 hundredths (almost half) of a standard deviation *below* that of the control group, which is desirable since *lower* values indicate *less* depression. You may recall from a statistics course that for all practical purposes, there are only three standard deviation units above and three below any mean for a normal distribution. Hence, for the mean of an experimental group to be about half of a standard deviation below the mean of the control group indicates a fairly substantial effect on a scale that can go (in the negative direction) from 0.00 to only –3.00.

There is no single set of generally accepted guidelines for interpreting values of *d*. Different reviewers may attach different labels to the same value. However, based on reading many meta-analyses, the interpretations of

---

[10] Note that some authors recommend "pooling" (a special type of averaging) of the standard deviations of both groups and using this pooled standard deviation as the divisor in calculating *d*.

various values that are commonly used have been identified and are shown in Box 11H.

Box 11H *Suggested interpretative terms to use when discussing values of* d.

Value of *d*	Interpretation in Words
0.00 to 0.20 or 0.00 to −0.20	no effect to small effect
0.21 to 0.33 or −0.21 to −0.33	small effect to moderate effect
0.34 to 0.50 or −0.34 to −0.50	moderate effect to strong effect
0.51 to 0.75 or −0.51 to −0.75	strong effect
0.76 and up or −0.76 and down	very strong effect

In the report of a meta-analysis, all the means, standard deviations, and numbers of cases should be reported. In addition, all the values of *d* should be reported: −0.45, −0.35, and −0.20. If there are a large number of studies, the values should be reported in a table. Their strengths can be discussed using the terms shown in Box 11H.

To average the values of *d* properly, we need to take into account that some studies have larger numbers of participants than others, so we should compute a *weighted* average. To do this, simply multiply each value of *d* by the total number of participants (*n*) in the study (total the number in the experimental group and the number in the control group). Finally, total the values in the last column, which is shown in Box 11I.

Box 11I *Preliminary steps in getting a weighted average of* d *(steps: 1. multiply* d *times* n, *2. total the number of participants, and 3. total the products in the last column)*:

	Value of *d*	×	Number of participants (*n*)	=	
Study 1	−0.45		30		−13.50
Study 2	−0.35		75		−26.25
Study 3	−0.20		230		−46.00
			Sum = 335		Sum = −85.75

To get the weighted average value of *d* across the three studies, divide the sum of the last column by the sum of the number of subjects as shown here: **−85.75/335 = −0.26**. Using the interpretative statements shown in Box 11H, we can say that the overall effect size as indicated by the weighted average value of *d* is "small to moderate."

Note that a "small effect" can be important. For instance, if a meta-analysis showed a small decrease in the incidence of cancer resulting from a simple change in diet (such as *d* = 0.21), the result would be important.

For a sample literature review in which Cohen's *d* is used as the primary measure of effect size, see Model Literature Review 3 near the end of this book.

✎ Guideline 11.10

Meta-analyses are often conducted by averaging correlation coefficients.

As you may know from your previous statistics course, the Pearson *r* is the most commonly used correlation coefficient. It is expressed on a scale from −1.00 (a perfect inverse relationship) through 0.00 (total absence of a relationship) to +1.00 (a perfect direct relationship). The value of *r* is interpreted by squaring it and multiplying the square by 100%. For instance, if we calculated an *r* of 0.72 for the relationship between height and weight, its square is $0.72 \times 0.72 = 0.52 \times 100\% = 52\%$, which means that 52% of the differences in weight can be accounted for by the differences in height among the sample.

Since *r* is already expressed on a standardized scale (from −1.00 to +1.00), we can refer to values of *r* to talk about relationships between variables measured on diverse scales (such as pounds for weight and inches for height). Thus, like *d* (see the previous guideline), *r* is a measure of "effect size" (i.e., magnitude).

Consider this example: Suppose we collect dozens of studies in which scores on reading comprehension tests have been correlated with scores on math word problem tests and values of *r* are reported in each. For the meta-analysis, we would report the values of *r* for the individual studies. For an overall, combined average, however, we need to perform a few calculations. The steps are:[11]

1. Convert each value of *r* to a value of *z* using Table 1 near the end of this book.
2. Multiply each value of *z* by the number of participants in the study.
3. Total the values of *z*.
4. Divide the sum of Step 3 by the number of values of *z*.
5. Convert the *z* found in Step 4 back to *r*, using Table 1 again.

To illustrate these steps, let us assume that there are only two studies with relevant values of *r*, which are shown in Box 11J along with other statistics. Total the values in the last column (48.65 + 97.02 = **145.67**) and total the number in the samples (50 + 140 = **190**). Then divide this sum by the total number in the combined samples: 145.67/190 = **0.767**. At this point, we have the weighted average value of *z* (0.767). To express this as the weighted average correlation coefficient, refer to Table 1 again and read from the *z* column moving left to the *r* column. In this case, you will find that a *z* of 0.767 corresponds to an *r* of **0.645**. Thus, we could report that the

---

[11] Note that the method shown here is the *approximate method*. To use the precise method, subtract 3 (a constant for all studies) from the number in each sample before multiplying by the value of *z*. Then follow the steps shown above, but perform the final division by the sum of the same sizes minus 3 for each sample. The approximate method and the precise method usually yield very similar results. For our particular sample, the result using the precise method is exactly the same as the result using the approximate method: 0.645.

weighted average value of r across studies is 0.645, with an underlying sample of 190 participants.

Box 11J *Values of r, corresponding values of z from Table 1. Multiply values of z by the numbers of subjects. Total the last column.*

	Value of r	Corresponding value of z from Table 1 (page 191)	times	Number in the sample	equals	
Study 1	0.75	0.973	×	50	=	48.65
Study 2	0.60	0.693	×	140	=	97.02

✑ Guideline 11.11

Consider using only correlation coefficients in your meta-analysis (after converting values of d to r).

Correlation coefficients are much more widely taught than Cohen's d in introductory statistics textbooks. Hence, it will be easier for many audiences if you report the weighted average value of r instead of the weighted average value of d as the mathematical synthesis in your meta-analysis.

Another reason for considering the exclusive reporting of values of r is that some of the studies that you have collected may report pairs of means (permitting you to calculate d) and others may report values of r. In this circumstance, if you convert all the values of d to r, you can report one grand weighted average of r for all the studies you have collected.

Converting values of d to r is easily accomplished by using Table 2 near the end of this book. For instance, Table 2 shows that a d equal to 1.4 corresponds to an r of 0.573. After converting the values of d to values of r using this simple process, calculate the weighted average value of r (as illustrated under Guideline 11.10), and report it as the final product of your mathematical synthesis.[12]

---

[12] Reporting Cohen's d is becoming more common. As more people learn its meaning, Guideline 11.11 will become less desirable.

Note that many instructors may prefer that you use *d* instead of *r*, especially if all (or almost all) of your literature contains means (such as means for experimental groups and means for control groups).

☙ Guideline 11.12
Because the results of meta-analyses are only as valid as the studies that underlie them, comment on the overall quality of the studies included in a meta-analysis.

If you have selected a topic for review on which the research is weak, the results of your meta-analysis should be interpreted in very tentative terms. On the other hand, there are topics on which there have been a large number of studies of high quality. The results of a meta-analysis based on such a topic should have high validity and the added advantage of being based on large numbers of participants.

Concluding Comments

Some researchers argue that a meta-analysis is superior to a highly qualitative (narrative) literature review because the mathematics used in a meta-analysis are "objective." However, if you consider the guidelines in this chapter and read Model Literature Review 3, you will see that even those who conduct meta-analyses must make subjective judgments such as whether to exclude methodologically weak studies, deciding which databases to search and which terms to use, and so on. In short, while the mathematical procedures produce an objective result, those who conduct meta-analyses should employ good judgment when deciding which studies to include and how to discuss the results.

The mathematical procedures in this chapter are presented for those who wish to conduct a basic meta-analysis, either as the heart of a highly quantitative literature review *or* as a subsection of a basically qualitative review. All college-level students need to understand the basic concepts of "effect size" and "meta-analysis" (i.e., an analysis in which effect sizes are averaged). The two most common statistics used to express effect size are *d* and *r*. You will *not* be asked to perform a meta-analysis in the following exercise because many of you are probably qualitatively oriented and will not need to perform one. However, essential concepts that underlie the technique will be covered because you will encounter reports of meta-analyses in your professional literature.

Exercise for Chapter 11

1. According to this chapter, a meta-analysis is an analysis that "transcends others" by doing what?

2. Suppose Researcher A found that 50% of a sample of 200 college freshmen knew that there are nine justices on the Supreme Court of the United States while Researcher B found that 60% of a sample of 400 college freshmen knew this fact. Very briefly explain why it would be inappropriate to add 50% and 60% to get 110% and divide by 2 for an average percentage of 55%.

3. According to this chapter, what is a "major advantage" of meta-analysis?

4. According to this chapter, should it be easy to tell from the beginning paragraphs whether a literature review is highly quantitative or highly qualitative? Explain.

5. Are you more likely to find a detailed description of how the search for literature was conducted in a qualitatively oriented literature review *or* in a meta-analysis?

6. Those who conduct meta-analyses are often concerned about the possibility of the "file drawer" effect (also known as a "publication bias"). Very briefly define this term.

7. Guideline 11.5 indicates that a reviewer should decide whether to exclude methodologically weak studies from his or her meta-analysis. If you will be conducting a meta-analysis, do you plan to exclude such studies? Explain.

8. Suppose someone was reviewing the literature on treatment programs for those who have committed physical spousal abuse. Would you recommend using gender as a moderator variable? Explain.

9. Suppose you read that the value of Cohen's *d* in an experiment was 0.22. How would you interpret this value?

10. If you will be conducting a meta-analysis, do you anticipate using Cohen's *d or* a correlation coefficient (*r*)? Explain.

11. According to this chapter, are those who conduct meta-analyses purely objective in their work?

12. If you will be conducting a highly *qualitative* review, have you learned anything in this chapter that will help you? Explain.

References

Akinbami, L. J., Cheng, T. L., & Kornfeld, D. (2001). A review of teen–tot programs: Comprehensive clinical care for young parents and their children. *Adolescence, 36*, 381–393.

American Psychological Association. (2001). *Publication Manual of the American Psychological Association* (5th ed.). Washington, DC: American Psychological Association.

Balasubramanian, S. K., & Cole, C. (2002). Consumers' search and use of nutrition information: The challenge and promise of the Nutrition Labeling and Information Act. *Journal of Marketing, 66*, 112–127.

Blok, H., Oostdam, R., Otter, M. E., & Overmaat, M. (2002). Computer-assisted instruction in support of beginning reading instruction: A review. *Review of Educational Research, 72*, 101–130.

Bloomer, S. R., Sipe, T. A., & Ruedt, D. E. (2002). Child support payment and child visitation: Perspectives from nonresident fathers and resident mothers. *Journal of Sociology and Social Welfare, XXIX*, 77–91.

Campbell, W. K., Foster, C. A., & Finkel, E. J. (2002). Does self-love lead to love for others?: A story of narcissistic game playing. *Journal of Personality & Social Psychology, 83*, 340–354.

Carlsmith, K. M., Darley, J. M., & Robinson, P. H. (2002). Why do we punish?: Deterrence and just deserts as motives for punishment. *Journal of Personality & Social Psychology, 83*, 284–299.

Cheng, T. (2002). Welfare recipients: How do they become independent? *Social Work Research, 26*, 159–170.

Christopherson, N., Janning, M., McConnell, E. D. (2002). Two kicks forward, one kick back: A content analysis of media discourses on the 1999 Women's World Cup Soccer Championship. *Sociology of Sport Journal, 19*, 170–188.

Cook, F. L., Barabas, J., & Page, B. I. (2002). Invoking Public Opinion: Policy elites and social security. *Public Opinion Quarterly, 66*, 235–264.

Dale, E. (personal communication with the author, April 1977).

Dirks, K. T., & Ferrin, D. L. (2002). Trust in leadership: Meta-analytic findings and implications for research and practice. *Journal of Applied Psychology, 87*, 611–628.

Dowson, M., & McInerney, D. M. (2001). Psychological parameters of students' social and work avoidance goals: A qualitative investigation. *Journal of Educational Psychology, 93*, 35–42.

Drigotas, S. M., Rusbult, C. E., & Verette, J. (1999). Level of commitment, mutuality of commitment, and couple well-being. *Personal Relationships, 6*, 389–409.

Duggan, C. H., & Dijkers, M. (2001). Quality of life after spinal cord injury: A qualitative study. *Rehabilitation Psychology, 46*, 3–27.

Elfenbein, H. A., & Ambady, N. (2002). On the universality and cultural specificity of emotion recognition: A meta-analysis. *Psychological Bulletin, 128*, 203–235.

Elliot, L., Foster, S., & Stinson, M. (2002). Student study habits using notes from a speech-to-text support service. *Exceptional Children, 69*, 25–40.

Frank, E., & Brandstaetter, V. (2002). Approach versus avoidance: Different types of commitment in intimate relationships. *Journal of Personality & Social Psychology, 82,* 208–221.

Franze, S. E., Foster, M., Abbott-Shim, M., McCarty, F., & Lambert, R. (2002). Describing Head Start family service workers: An examination of factors related to job satisfaction, empowerment, and multiculturalism. *Families in Society: The Journal of Contemporary Human Services, 83,* 257–264.

Gomez, M. J., Fassinger, R. E., Prosser, J., Cooke, K., Mejia, B., & Luna, J. (2001). Voces abriendo caminos (voices foraging paths): A qualitative study of the career development of notable Latinas. *Journal of Counseling Psychology, 48,* 286–300.

Griffin, E. (1994). *A first look at communication theory* (2nd Ed.). New York: McGraw-Hill, Inc.

Grusec, J. E. (1992). Social learning theory and developmental psychology: The legacies of Robert Sears and Albert Bandura. *Developmental Psychology, 28,* 776–786.

Harris, R. A. (2001). *The plagiarism handbook: Strategies for preventing, detecting, and dealing with plagiarism.* Los Angeles: Pyrczak Publishing.

Harris, R. A. (2003). *Writing with clarity and style: A guide to rhetorical devices for contemporary writers.* Los Angeles: Pyrczak Publishing.

Hausenblas, H. A., Nigg, C. R., Downs, D. S., Fleming, D. S., & Connaughton, D. P. (2002). Perceptions of exercise stages, barrier self-efficacy, and decisional balance for middle-level school students. *Journal of Early Adolescence, 22,* 436–454.

Henderlong, J., & Lepper, M. R. (2002). The effects of praise on children's intrinsic motivation: A review and synthesis. *Psychological Bulletin, 128,* 774–795.

Hionidou, V. (2002). Why do people die in famines? Evidence from three island populations. *Population Studies, 56,* 65–80.

Hunter, K. G. (2002). An application of herd theory to interest group behavior. *Administration & Society, 34,* 389–410.

Kegler, M. C., McCormick, L., Crawford, M., Allen, P., Spigner, C., & Ureda, J. (2002). An exploration of family influences on smoking among ethnically diverse adolescents. *Health Education & Behavior, 29,* 473–490.

Kuncel, N. R., Hezlett, S. A., & Ones, D. S. (2001). A comprehensive meta-analysis of the predictive validity of the Graduate Record Examinations: Implications for graduate student selection and performance. *Psychological Bulletin, 127,* 162–181.

Locke, E. A., & Latham, G. P. (2002). Building a practically useful theory of goal setting and task motivation. *American Psychologist, 57,* 705–717.

Loneck, B., Banks, S., Way, B., & Bonaparte, E. (2002). An empirical model of therapeutic process for psychiatric emergency room clients with dual disorders. *Social Work Research, 26,* 132–144.

Lupton, R. A., & Chapman, K. J. (2002). Russian and American college students' attitudes, perceptions, and tendencies towards cheating. *Educational Research, 44,* 17–27.

Lydon, J. E. (1996). Toward a theory of commitment. (In C. Seligman, J. Olson, & M. Zanna (Eds.), *Values: The Eighth Ontario Symposium* (pp. 191–213). Hillsdale, NJ: Erlbaum.)

McKay, J. R., Pettinati, H. M., Morrison, R., Feeley, M., Mulvaney, F. D., & Gallop, R. (2002). Relation of depression diagnoses to 2-year outcomes in cocaine-dependent patients in a randomized continuing care study. *Psychology of Addictive Behaviors, 16*, 225–235.

Merriam-Webster Unabridged Dictionary [electronic version]. (2002). Springfield, MA: Merriam Webster.

Pinto, R. M. (2002). Social work values, welfare reform, and immigrant citizenship conflicts. *Families in Society: The Journal of Contemporary Human Services, 83*, 85–92.

Porta, C., Handelman, E., & McGovern, P. (1999). Needlestick injuries among health care workers: A Literature Review. *AAOHN Journal, 47*, 237–244.

Purdie, N., Hattie, J., & Carroll, A. (2002). A review of the research on interventions for Attention Deficit Hyperactivity Disorder: What works best? *Review of Educational Research, 72*, 61–99.

Rhee, S. H., & Waldman, I. D. (2002). Genetic and environmental influences on antisocial behavior: A meta-analysis of twin and adoption studies. *Psychological Bulletin, 128*, 490–529.

Rhoades, L., & Eisenberger, R. (2002). Perceived organizational support: A review of the literature. *Journal of Applied Psychology, 87*, 698–714.

Torres-Reyna, O., & Shapiro, R. Y. (2002). The polls–trends: Defense and the military. *Public Opinion Quarterly, 66*, 279–303.

Schmitz, C. L., Wagner, J. D., & Menke, E. M. (2001). The interconnection of childhood poverty and homelessness: Negative impact/points of access. *Families in Society: The Journal of Contemporary Human Services, 82*, 69–77.

Somers, M. J. (1995). Organizational commitment, turnover and absenteeism: An examination of direct and interaction effects. *Journal of Organizational Behavior, 16*, 49–58.

Unger, J. B., Gallaher, P., Shakib, S., Ritt-Olson, A., Palmer, P. H., & Johnson, C. A. (2002). The AHIMSA Acculturation Scale: A new measure of acculturation for adolescents in a multicultural society. *Journal of Early Adolescence, 22*, 225–251.

Van Lange, P. A. M., Rusbult, C. E., Drigotas, S. M., Arriaga, X. B., Witcher, B. S., & Cox, C. L. (1997). Willingness to sacrifice in close relationships. *Journal of Personality and Social Psychology, 72*, 1373–1395.

Wasti, S. A., & Cortina, L. M. (2002). Coping in context: Sociocultural determinants of responses to sexual harassment. *Journal of Personality & Social Psychology, 83*, 394–405.

Wood, S. J., Murdock, J. Y., & Cronin, M. E. (2002). Self-monitoring and at-risk middle school students. *Behavior Modification, 26*, 605–626.

Zechmeister, J. S., & Romero, C. (2002). Victim and offender accounts of interpersonal conflict: Autobiographical narratives of forgiveness and unforgiveness. *Journal of Personality & Social Psychology, 82*, 675–686.

Appendix A

Checklist of Guidelines

Instructors may want to refer to the following checklist numbers when commenting on students' writing. Students can use this checklist to review important points as they prepare their literature reviews.

Chapter 1 Qualitative versus Quantitative Reviews

____ 1.1 In quantitatively oriented literature reviews, precise statistical results from the literature are presented and sometimes mathematically combined.

____ 1.2 If the main thrust of a review is the mathematical combination of results of various studies by various researchers, the result is called a meta-analysis or meta-analytic review.

____ 1.3 In qualitatively oriented reviews, statistical studies are often described in general terms, but precise statistical values are de-emphasized.

____ 1.4 Both types of reviews have many common features.

____ 1.5 Many literature reviews are a blend of qualitatively oriented and quantitatively oriented approaches.

____ 1.6 Distinguish between qualitative and quantitative *literature reviews* and qualitative and quantitative *empirical research*.

____ 1.7 Read both qualitatively oriented and quantitatively oriented reviews in preparation for writing a review.

Chapter 2 Selecting a Topic for Review

____ 2.1 Consider carefully your audience's expectations and/or requirements when selecting a topic.

____ 2.2 When selecting a topic, emphasize your audience's expectations and requirements instead of your personal interests.

____ 2.3 Put possible topics *in writing*. If your professor is your audience, ask him or her to examine your written topic ideas.

____ 2.4 Consider brainstorming a list of possible topics.

____ 2.5 Consider starting by initially selecting broad topics and then narrowing them by adding delimitations.

____ 2.6 Scan titles (and abstracts) of articles in your topic area early in the process of selecting a topic.

____ 2.7 Consider selecting a topic on which there is theoretical literature.

____ 2.8 Consider selecting a theory as the topic for a literature review.

___ 2.9   Consider preliminary definitions of the terms in the topics you are considering.

___ 2.10   If your literature review will introduce your original empirical research, strive for a close fit between the topic(s) reviewed and the variables studied in your research.

___ 2.11   Consider your orientation and whether a topic you are considering lends itself more to qualitative or quantitative analysis.

___ 2.12   Consider reviewing the literature on instrument(s) or assessment procedure(s).

___ 2.13   Select a topic with an eye toward your future goals and activities.

Chapter 3   Searching for Literature and Refining the Topic

___ 3.1   Invest time in learning how to conduct advanced searches of a database.

___ 3.2   Familiarize yourself with the Boolean operators: NOT, AND, and OR.

___ 3.3   Consider using demographics to delimit your search.

___ 3.4   Consider searching for theoretical literature on your topic.

___ 3.5   Examine the references cited in the literature that you locate.

___ 3.6   Search for the names of prominent individuals who have written on your topic.

___ 3.7   Consider using "history" as a term in your search.

___ 3.8   Consider using "definition" as a term in your search.

___ 3.9   Consider using an exact phrase match.

___ 3.10   Consider using truncated terms or wildcards to locate literature that is classified under a derivative term.

___ 3.11   When you want to narrow your search to the most relevant literature, consider restricting your search to the title and/or abstract.

___ 3.12   Consider using the word "review" in your search in order to find previous literature reviews on your topic.

___ 3.13   Consider searching for the term "qualitative."

___ 3.14   Consider searching a citation index.

___ 3.15   Maintain a written record of how you conducted your literature search.

Chapter 4   Retrieving and Evaluating Information from the Web

___ 4.1   FedStats is one of the most valuable sources of statistical information on the Web.

___ 4.2   State and local governments and their agencies (including state-supported universities) often post very current statistics on the Web.

___ 4.3   Use the raw statistics from governmental agencies—not statistics filtered by politicians or others with special interests.

___   4.4   Consider consulting the Library of Congress' Virtual Reference Shelf on the Web.

___   4.5   Consider accessing information posted on the Web by a variety of nongovernmental agencies, associations, and advocacy groups.

___   4.6   Major search engines used by the public at large often provide helpful information for use in academic literature reviews.

___   4.7   Pay attention to the extension (gov, edu, org, com, and net) in the results of Web searches.

___   4.8   Consider clicking on "cached" when opening a Web site from a search engine.

___   4.9   When you find a Web site that is very useful, consider following the links, if any, that it provides.

Chapter 5   Taking Notes and Avoiding Unintentional Plagiarism

___   5.1   Common knowledge does not need to be cited, but original expressions of it should be cited.

___   5.2   Even if you cite the ideas of others rephrased in your own words, the original source should be cited.

___   5.3   Failure to indicate clearly the beginning *and* end of summarized literature may lead to charges of plagiarism.

___   5.4   Establish criteria for the inclusion of literature in your review.

___   5.5   Give each piece of literature a unique identifier such as the surname of the first author.

___   5.6   While taking notes, consider building a table that summarizes key points in the literature you are reviewing.

___   5.7   Consider using color-coding while reading and making notes.

___   5.8   Pay special attention to definitions while taking notes.

___   5.9   Pay special attention to researchers' descriptions of the limitations of their research methodology.

___   5.10 It is misleading to read and make notes only on the abstracts of articles without disclosing the fact that you have done so in your review.

___   5.11 Make notes on how other writers have organized the literature on your topic.

Chapter 6   Guidelines for Evaluating Sources of Literature

___   6.1   Even the most prestigious sources sometimes publish seriously flawed material.

___   6.2   Consider who sponsors a publication. Professional associations, foundations, government agencies, and for-profit companies are major sponsors.

___   6.3   Check to see whether a journal (or publisher) has an independent editorial board.

___   6.4   Check to see whether a journal uses a "blind" peer-review process when selecting manuscripts for publication. (This is also called a "juried process.")

___   6.5   Consider the institutional affiliation of the author.

___ 6.6   Consider the overall quality of a journal in which an article is published.

___ 6.7   Journals that publish long articles are usually more important sources than those that publish short ones.

Chapter 7   Evaluating and Interpreting Research Literature

___ 7.1   Be wary of any source claiming to offer "proof."

___ 7.2   Research is almost always flawed by inadequate samples.

___ 7.3   Be cautious when a body of literature has a common sampling flaw.

___ 7.4   Research is almost always flawed by inadequate measures.

___ 7.5   Consider the reliability of measures used in research.

___ 7.6   Consider the validity of measures used in research.

___ 7.7   Consider the authors' self-critique of their own research methods.

___ 7.8   Be cautious when a researcher refers to causality.

___ 7.9   Assess the strength of trends across studies when evaluating literature.

___ 7.10 Recognize the limitations of significance testing.

Chapter 8   Planning and Writing the First Draft

___ 8.1   Before preparing an outline, review your notes and group them according to content.

___ 8.2   When beginning to build a topic outline, consider the order in which other writers have presented material on your topic.

___ 8.3   Consider your first topic outline as a tentative one that is subject to change.

___ 8.4   Consider filling in your outline with brief notes (including unique identifiers) before beginning to write your review.

___ 8.5   Establish the importance of the topic that you are reviewing in the introductory paragraphs of your review.

___ 8.6   Avoid vague references to statistics—especially in the first paragraph of your review.

___ 8.7   Provide specific definitions of major variables early in the literature review.

___ 8.8   Write an essay that moves logically from one point to another. Do not write a string of annotations.

___ 8.9   When they are available, use more than one reference to support a point you make. However, do not cite very long strings of references for a single point.

___ 8.10 Use quotations sparingly. Instead write the literature review using your own words.

___ 8.11 Explicitly state what you think are reasonable conclusions based on the literature for each major subtopic that you cover.

___ 8.12   Consider theories and/or models when reaching conclusions.

___ 8.13   Critique the research you cite, which will help you show your readers why you have reached particular conclusions.

___ 8.14   Point out gaps in the literature, explain why they are important, and mention them in your conclusions.

Chapter 9   Revising and Refining the First Draft

___ 9.1   Recheck headings and subheadings. Modify and/or add or delete as necessary.

___ 9.2   Check to see that all your paragraphs are straightforward and reasonably short.

___ 9.3   Check to see that you have used rhetorical questions sparingly.

___ 9.4   Consider using transitional terms to make one paragraph flow from the previous one.

___ 9.5   If more than one paragraph is based on the same reference, use wording that makes it clear.

___ 9.6   Avoid beginning your literature review with truisms.

___ 9.7   Consider using a first paragraph that provides historical context—if the context is clearly on-target and interesting.

___ 9.8   Remove any material that is meant to be clever or amusing.

___ 9.9   Revise to reduce the amount of anecdotal material.

___ 9.10   When using the Harvard method for citation, it is often better to emphasize content over authorship.

___ 9.11   Cross-check the references cited in the body of your review against those in your reference list at the end.

___ 9.12   Have your first draft critiqued by others. Pay careful attention to their criticisms and begin with the assumption that they are correct if they give you negative feedback.

Chapter 10   Blending Qualitative and Quantitative Approaches

___ 10.1   Consider your audience's needs for reporting specific statistics in your literature review.

___ 10.2   If you fail to state that a difference or relationship is statistically significant, your readers will assume that it is, which is acceptable if this is true.

___ 10.3   Consider pointing out especially large (or strong) and especially small (or weak) differences or relationships.

___ 10.4   Examine your literature review to identify vague terms that refer to quantities, and consider replacing them with specific statistics.

___ 10.5   Consider summarizing key statistics in a table.

___ 10.6   Avoid overburdening readers with statistics in the narrative of your review.

___ 10.7 If a particular statistic is especially important in helping you to create a synthesis, consider commenting on the quality of the study that generated the statistic.

___ 10.8 Consider using wording that indicates which statements are based on statistical information and which are not.

___ 10.9 Consider discussing the statistical support, if any, for important theories that you describe in your literature review.

Chapter 11 Preparing a Meta-Analysis

___ 11.1 A meta-analysis of results presented as percentages in various studies can be conducted by calculating a weighted average of the percentages.

___ 11.2 The beginning of a meta-analysis should be similar to the beginning of a qualitative review.

___ 11.3 When writing a meta-analysis, indicate the search terms you used as well as the databases that you searched.

___ 11.4 Consider discussing efforts made to overcome the "file drawer" effect (i.e., publication bias) on the outcome(s) of your meta-analysis.

___ 11.5 Decide whether you will exclude methodologically weak studies from your meta-analysis.

___ 11.6 If some studies are excluded from the meta-analysis for reasons other than weak methodology, provide specific reasons and/or criteria for their exclusion.

___ 11.7 Consider including one or more moderator variables in your meta-analysis. If they are included, provide a rationale for their selection.

___ 11.8 Because a meta-analysis typically can be conducted on only some of the literature on a topic, consider incorporating a meta-analysis within a larger qualitative review.

___ 11.9 Meta-analyses are often conducted by standardizing the difference between means using Cohen's d.

___ 11.10 Meta-analyses are often conducted by averaging correlation coefficients.

___ 11.11 Consider using only correlation coefficients in your meta-analysis (after converting values of d to r).

___ 11.12 Because the results of meta-analyses are only as valid as the studies that underlie them, comment on the overall quality of the studies included in a meta-analysis.

Appendix B

Qualitative versus Quantitative Research

Mildred L. Patten

As you can probably guess, **quantitative research** is research in which the results are presented as quantities or numbers (that is, statistics) and **qualitative research** is research in which the results are trends or themes that are described in words. However, this is an oversimplification since there are many features that distinguish the two types. To understand some of the major differences, let's consider an example.

Suppose a metropolitan police force is demoralized—with signs of high rates of absenteeism, failure to follow procedures, and so on. Furthermore, the press has raised questions about the effectiveness of the force and its leadership. In such a situation, the police commission might call in a researcher who is assigned the task of identifying possible causes and solutions.

If a quantitative researcher is retained, she would probably begin with a review of the research literature on demoralized police departments. From the review, she would attempt to develop hypotheses to be explored in her research. This is a *deductive approach* to planning the research, that is, she is deducing from the literature possible explanations (that is, hypotheses) to be tested in the research. In contrast, a qualitative researcher would tend to use an *inductive approach* to planning the research. He might, for example, begin to gather data on the specific police force in question and use the very early, preliminary findings as a basis for planning other research activities. In fact, *some* qualitative researchers consciously avoid considering previous research since it might color the way they look at a given situation.

When deciding what types of instruments (that is, measuring tools) to use, a quantitative researcher would tend to emphasize those that produce data that can quickly be reduced to numbers such as structured questionnaires or interview schedules with objective formats such as multiple-choice questions. In contrast, a qualitative researcher would tend to emphasize instruments that yield words such as unstructured interviews or direct, unstructured observations of police force officers and their administrators.

When deciding which members of the force to use as subjects, a quantitative researcher would tend to se-

lect a large sample, which is made possible within a limited research budget by objective instruments such as an anonymous, objective questionnaire that takes little time to administer.[1] A qualitative researcher will tend to select a small sample for the reverse reason.

When conducting the research, a quantitative researcher would tend to spend a little time directly interacting with the subjects (largely because the nature of her instruments do not require it). A qualitative researcher, on the other hand, might spend a considerable amount of time interviewing and observing various members of the force over an extended period.

While working with the subjects,[2] a qualitative researcher would be open to the possibility of making adjustments in the instruments such as reformulating questions or adding questions based on earlier responses by subjects. A quantitative researcher would seldom make such adjustments.

Also, a quantitative researcher would tend to summarize all responses with statistics and seldom report on individual subjects. A qualitative researcher would tend to cite individuals' responses (such as quoting individual subjects) in the results section of a report.

Finally, a quantitative researcher would tend to generalize her results to one or more populations, while a qualitative researcher would tend to limit his conclusions to individuals who were directly studied.

Should the police commission select a quantitative or qualitative researcher? Some of the criteria that should be considered when making such a decision are:

A. Some research questions inherently lend themselves more to the quantitative or qualitative approach.

---

[1] In addition, she will usually attempt to select a *random sample* in which all subjects have an equal chance of being selected; this can be done, for example, by drawing names out of a hat. The uses of random samples and their relationship to statistics are discussed in later topics. A qualitative researcher is more likely to select a *purposive* sample of people she believes are key in terms of social dynamics, leadership, etc.

[2] Note that quantitative researchers tend to use the terms "subjects" or "respondents" whereas qualitative researchers tend to use the term "participants."

For example, "What is the impact of AIDS on the U.S. economy?" is a question that lends itself to quantitative research since the economy is usually measured with numbers. On the other hand, "What is the emotional impact of AIDS on at-risk health care workers?" is a question that lends itself more to the qualitative approach than the first question since it focuses on emotional impact—although it could be examined with either qualitative or quantitative research depending on the orientation of the researcher.

B. When little is known about a topic, qualitative research usually should be initially favored. New topics are constantly emerging in all fields: new diseases such as HIV, new crimes such as car-jacking, and new educational techniques such as putting students on the Internet. On new topics, there will be very little, if any, research literature and, perhaps, no theory with direct applications. In their absence, quantitative researchers may find it difficult to employ the deductive approach. Also, quantitative researchers might find it difficult to write structured questions about a little-known topic. How can you know exactly what to ask when you know little about a topic? In contrast, a qualitative researcher could start with broad questions and refine them during the course of the interviews as various themes and issues start to emerge. Based on the qualitative results, theories might be developed from which hypotheses could be deduced and subsequently tested by quantitative research.

C. When the subjects belong to a culture that is closed or secretive, qualitative research should usually be favored. A skilled qualitative researcher who is willing to spend considerable time breaking through the barriers that keep researchers out is more likely to be successful than a quantitative researcher who tends to spend less time interacting with subjects.

D. When potential subjects are not available for extensive interactions or observation, the quantitative approach should be considered. For example, it might be difficult to schedule extensive interviews with chief executives of major corporations.

E. When time and funds are very limited, quantitative research might be favored. This is an arguable criterion. However, it is suggested because quantitative research can often provide a quick, inexpensive snapshot of a narrow aspect of a problem. Qualitative methods do not lend themselves to the snapshot approach.

F. When the audience (such as legislators or funding agencies) requires "hard numbers," quantitative research should be favored or, at least, incorporated into a qualitative research project. When someone says, "Just the numbers, please," themes and trends illustrated with quotations are unlikely to impress. For such an audience, one should, when possible, start by presenting statistics. This might open the door to consideration of more qualitative considerations. Notice that implicit in this criterion is the notion that both qualitative and quantitative approaches might be used in a given research project, with each approach contributing a different type of information.

Up to this point, we have been considering quantitative and qualitative research as though they are opposites. However, some researchers conduct research that is a blend of the two approaches. For example, a quantitative researcher who uses semistructured interviews to collect data, reduces the data to statistics, but also reports quotations from subjects to support the statistics, is conducting research that has some of the characteristics of both approaches.

As you can see, our hypothetical police commission needs to make a complex decision. How would you answer the question regarding the type of research the police commission should request? Arguably, a combination of both approaches might be the best answer.

Model Literature Review 1

The Performance of Narcissists Rises and Falls with Perceived Opportunity for Glory

Harry M. Wallace
Case Western Reserve University

Roy F. Baumeister
Case Western Reserve University

Editorial notes: The paragraphs in this literature review have been numbered to make it easy to refer to specific portions of this review during classroom discussions. The numbers are italicized superscripts, which appear at the beginning of each paragraph. All other superscripts, if any, refer to footnotes within the review.

This review was written as an introduction to a report on original research conducted by the authors. Only the literature review portion of the report is reprinted here. Note that all the other sample literature reviews in this book were written as "stand-alone" reviews—not as introductions to original research.

[1]Andre, a pass receiver for his football team, has a reputation as a flashy player who makes difficult, spectacular plays at crucial times in important games. When the stakes are high and the spotlight is bright, Andre is at his best. Andre has also developed a reputation as a malcontent who complains when the ball is not thrown to him. On one infamous occasion, Andre nearly started a fight with his quarterback for throwing the ball to another player—even though the pass was caught for a touchdown that won the game. Andre also has a penchant for blowing easy plays, especially during practice and in games that are relatively insignificant. One of his teammates once explained to a reporter, "Andre is a real pain in the neck. He's chronically late to practice, he struts around like he's God's gift to football, and I don't think I've ever seen him throw a decent block for another player. But when the game is on the line, we're all happy to have Andre on our team." Why does Andre only perform well when the circumstances are most challenging? What can account for Andre's lack of consideration for his coach and fellow teammates? The present research offers an explanation: Andre might be a narcissist.[1]

[2]The present investigation examines the effects of narcissism on task performance. We hypothesized that narcissism can be either advantageous or detrimental to performance, depending on the situational context. Specifically, we reasoned that the effects of narcissism on task performance should be moderated by perceived self-enhancement opportunity. Narcissists crave opportunities for self-enhancement, and some tasks offer more self-enhancement value than others. Narcissists should perform well when task success will be taken as an impressive sign of personal superiority. However, when task success will be unimpressive, narcissists should perform relatively poorly. In comparison, the performance of people with low levels of narcissism should be less affected by perceived self-enhancement opportunity.

Narcissism and Performance

[3]In Greek mythology, Narcissus was a young man who fell in love with his own reflection in a pool and ultimately perished as a result of his self-absorption. In the terminology of modern clinical psychology, such excessive and dysfunctional self-love is characteristic of people with narcissistic personality disorder (see *Diagnostic and Statistical Manual of Mental Disorders*, 4th ed. [*DSM-IV*]; American Psychiatric Association, 1994). According to *DSM-IV* classification, people with narcissistic personality disorder exhibit an exaggerated sense of self-importance and uniqueness, arrogance, an unreasonable sense of entitlement, exploitative tendencies, empathy deficits, and a need for excessive admiration.

[4]The concept of narcissism has been extended from the restricted domain of mental illness to encompass many tendencies among ostensibly normal individuals. Empirical research on subclinical narcissism has flourished since the creation of the NPI (Raskin & Hall,

---

[1] We use the terms *narcissists* and *high narcissists* to refer to people with relatively high scores on the Narcissistic Personality Inventory (NPI; Raskin & Hall, 1979; Raskin & Terry, 1988), a measure of subclinical narcissism. The term *low narcissists* refers to people with relatively low scores on the NPI.

1979; Raskin & Terry, 1988), a self-report questionnaire that has become the standard measure of narcissism in normal populations. Empirical research using the NPI has shown that narcissistic people think highly of themselves and their abilities (Emmons, 1984; Gabriel, Critelli, & Ee, 1994; John & Robins, 1994; Raskin, Novacek, & Hogan, 1991a; Robins & Beer, 2001). This research also shows that narcissists have unusually high self-expectations (Farwell & Wohlwend-Lloyd, 1998) and an exaggerated sense of personal control over their world (Dhavale, 2000; Watson, Sawrie, & Biderman, 1991). High levels of self-confidence and self-efficacy have been linked with high achievement in past research (e.g., Bandura, 1977; Baumeister, Hamilton, & Tice, 1985; Feather, 1966, 1968; Tuckman & Sexton, 1992; see Pajares, 1997, for a review), so it is plausible that narcissism could facilitate performance success.

[5]To be sure, one might expect a positive correlation between performance and narcissism even if narcissism did not produce self-fulfilling expectancies of success. Performance success could foster narcissism. A history of performance success should gradually boost one's self-regard (Felson, 1993), which could fuel the development of narcissism. High performers might continue to perform well even as their levels of narcissism grow.

[6]Thus, there are good theoretical grounds for predicting that narcissists might outperform other people in general. Past studies examining possible links between narcissism and performance have produced conflicting results, however. Gabriel et al. (1994) found that narcissism was positively correlated with self-reported intelligence, but they found no correlation between narcissism and actual performance on an intelligence test. John and Robins (1994) found that narcissistic participants thought they performed quite well on a group interaction task, but observer evaluations indicated that narcissists performed no better or worse than others. Robins and John (1997) asked study participants to present a convincing oral argument to a group of people. People with high scores on narcissism rated their performances much higher than low scorers rated their performances. However, objective measures revealed no difference in the quality of presentations given by high and low narcissists. Raskin (1980) found that narcissism was positively correlated with both self-reported creativity and performance on an objective creativity test. Farwell and Wohlwend-Lloyd (1998) conducted two studies in which narcissistic students were more likely than their peers to overestimate their future and current course grades. Narcissism and course grades were positively correlated in one study, but no correlation between nar-

cissism and course grades was found in the other study. In sum, past research has demonstrated that narcissists consider themselves to be exceptional performers, but the actual performance of narcissists in past studies has often been no better than that of other people.

The Importance of Self-Enhancement Opportunity

[7]The preceding section reveals a discrepancy. Theoretical grounds and narcissists' self-appraisals suggest that narcissism ought to improve performance, but most studies of actual performance quality have failed to find any benefit of narcissism. One possible explanation for this discrepancy is that narcissism simply makes mediocre performers think they are superior to others. The failure of confidence and self-fulfilling expectancies of success to produce any actual performance improvement would be somewhat surprising, but otherwise this explanation could account for the discrepancy between subjective and objective benefits.

[8]The present investigation, however, is based on a more complex theory about the effects of narcissism on performance. We reasoned that the performance level of narcissists might rise or fall depending on the situational opportunity for self-enhancement. We define a performance situation as having high self-enhancement opportunity to the extent that successful performance will be interpreted as an indication that the performer has impressively high levels of skills, talents, or other desirable traits. In other words, self-enhancement opportunity denotes the degree to which one can potentially win glory by performing well.

[9]Most people seek to self-enhance to some degree, but narcissists are especially zealous in their pursuit of personal glory (e.g., Campbell, Reeder, Sedikides, & Elliot, 2000; John & Robins, 1994; Morf & Rhodewalt, 2001; Robins & Beer, 2001). Because narcissists are so obsessed with self-enhancement, they should be keenly aware that some performance tasks offer more potential for self-enhancement than others. When narcissists perceive that a performance task offers no opportunity for self-enhancement, their motivation to perform that task should be reduced, and their performance may suffer.

[10]At least three factors determine whether a performance is self-enhancing for the performer: (a) the quality of the performance, (b) audience characteristics, and (c) the diagnosticity of the performance task. The first factor is obvious: The self-enhancement value of performance increases with the quality of the performance. There is no glory to be gained by performing at a low level. The self-enhancement potential of a perform-

ance is also influenced by audience characteristics. A great public performance should be more self-enhancing than an equally great private performance. Moreover, a great performance witnessed by people whose opinions are valued by the performer should be more self-enhancing than a great performance witnessed by people the performer does not respect. Still, even a successful performance in front of a respected audience may not necessarily be self-enhancing. For the performance to be self-enhancing, it must be diagnostic of special achievement. Task success is not diagnostic of achievement when success is assumed or expected. Thus, challenging tasks offer more potential for self-enhancement than unchallenging tasks.

The Impact of Challenge Level

[11]When the task goal is introduced as a difficult challenge that people rarely achieve, narcissists should view this performance task as an excellent opportunity to demonstrate their superiority over others. Just as the mythical Narcissus was obsessed with observing his own reflected beauty, modern-day narcissists crave chances to observe their reflected greatness (Robins & John, 1997). As discussed earlier, difficult goal achievement is more diagnostic of exceptional ability than easy goal achievement. Narcissists' motivation to achieve difficult goals should be especially strong because they are more concerned with self-enhancement than other people (e.g., Campbell et al., 2000; John & Robins, 1994; Paulhus, 1998). Furthermore, narcissists' inflated self-views should give them confidence that they can succeed at tasks at which most others have failed. This combination of high motivation and high self-confidence should help their performance on challenging tasks. In contrast, high performance on an unchallenging task is not indicative of high ability, so narcissists may have relatively little motivation to exert themselves on such tasks. Narcissists' high self-expectations could even be detrimental to performance on unchallenging tasks. If narcissists believe task success is common, they may take it for granted.

[12]People who are not narcissistic are less concerned about self-enhancement than narcissists, so their motivation and performance should be less affected by the self-enhancement opportunity presented by the task goal. If the difficulty of a challenge has any effect on the performance of low narcissists, the effect should be in the opposite direction of the predicted effect of challenge level on the performance of narcissists. The motivation of low narcissists should vary little as a function of challenge level, but their confidence and performance could

suffer if they consider the task goal to be too challenging. When the task goal is unchallenging, low narcissists should have some confidence in their ability to succeed, but they should be less likely than narcissists to assume success.

[13]One reason why past studies have found no evidence of a relationship between narcissism and performance may be that the performance goals used in these studies were not challenging or unchallenging enough to reveal performance differences based on levels of narcissism. Although no previous research has directly addressed the relationship among narcissism, task challenge, and performance, past research on achievement motivation provides indirect support for the present hypotheses. Atkinson (1958) and Kukla (1972, 1974) demonstrated that confidence in one's abilities helps performance on difficult tasks and hurts performance on easy tasks. This performance pattern is apparently a function of motivation: Meyer (1987) found that people with very high self-rated ability reported that they would invest more effort on tasks of high difficulty than on tasks of low difficulty, whereas people with very low self-rated ability reported that they would invest more effort on tasks of low difficulty than on tasks of high difficulty. In addition, Trope (1979) found that persons with high perceived ability have a particularly strong preference for tasks of high diagnosticity, and, as he noted, difficult tasks are especially diagnostic for high ability levels. Narcissists clearly think highly of their abilities, so they should prefer to invest more effort on highly difficult tasks.

The Impact of Audience Evaluation

[14]The self-enhancement value of high performance should increase when an audience observes the performance. In general, people are more motivated to perform when others can evaluate their individual performance. For example, people exert less individual effort toward a group goal when the individual contributions of group members are unidentifiable, a phenomenon known as social loafing (e.g., Latane, Williams, & Harkins, 1979; Williams, Harkins, & Latane, 1981; see Karau & Williams, 1993, for a review). On collective group tasks, where the performances of individual group members are indistinguishable, potential for individual self-enhancement is limited because the glory associated with exceptional group performance is diffused among group members. If narcissists are strongly motivated to self-enhance, as past research suggests, they should be far more motivated to perform individual tasks than collective tasks. Thus, narcissists' self-serving orientation

could lead them to exhibit more social loafing than less narcissistic people exhibit.

[15]The relationship between narcissism and social loafing has not been explored, but recent research has shown that people who perceive themselves as better than others are more prone to social loafing than those who consider themselves average (Charbonnier, Huguet, Brauer, & Monteil, 1998; Huguet, Charbonnier, & Monteil, 1999). In addition, Sanna (1992) found that people with high self-efficacy performed well when their performance was being evaluated but that they performed poorly when they did not expect their performance to be evaluated. People with low self-efficacy showed the opposite pattern of performance. Narcissists consistently rate themselves as better than others (e.g., Farwell & Wohlwend-Lloyd, 1998; Gabriel et al., 1994; John & Robins, 1994; Raskin, 1980; Robins & John, 1997), and they have high self-efficacy (e.g., Farwell & Wohlwend-Lloyd, 1998; Watson et al., 1991), so they too should perform best in the presence of an evaluative audience.

Present Investigation

[16]In the present research, we examined the impact of self-enhancement opportunity on performance in four experiments. The central hypothesis was that objective performance quality depends on an interaction of narcissism and self-enhancement opportunity. More precisely, we expected that high narcissists would perform better when the opportunity for self-enhancement was high and salient than when no such opportunity was present, whereas low narcissists would exhibit either no difference or the opposite pattern.

References

American Psychiatric Association. (1994). *Diagnostic and statistical manual of mental disorders* (4th ed.). Washington, DC: Author.

Atkinson, J. W. (1958). Towards experimental analysis of human motivation in terms of motives, expectancies, and incentives. (In J. W. Atkinson (Ed.), *Motives in fantasy, action, and society: A method of assessment and study* (pp. 288–305). Princeton, NJ: Nostrand.)

Bandura, A. (1977). Self-efficacy: Toward a unifying theory of behavioral change. *Psychological Review, 84*, 191–215.

Baumeister, R. F., Hamilton, J. C., & Tice, D. M. (1985). Public versus private expectancy of success: Confidence booster or performance pressure? *Journal of Personality and Social Psychology, 48*, 1447–1457.

Campbell, W. K., Reeder, G. D., Sedikides, C., & Elliot, A. J. (2000). Narcissism and comparative self-enhancement strategies. *Journal of Research in Personality, 34*, 329–347.

Charbonnier, E., Huguet, P., Brauer, M., & Monteil, J. (1998). Social loafing and self-beliefs: People's collective effort depends on the extent to which they distinguish themselves as better than others. *Social Behavior and Personality, 26*, 329–340.

Dhavale, D. (2000). *Narcissism and irrational positive beliefs.* (Unpublished master's thesis, Case Western Reserve University)

Emmons, R. A. (1984). Factor analysis and construct validity of the Narcissistic Personality Inventory. *Journal of Personality Assessment, 48*, 291–300.

Farwell, L., & Wohlwend-Lloyd, R. (1998). Narcissistic processes: Optimistic expectations, favorable self-evaluations, and self-enhancing attributions. *Journal of Personality, 66*, 65–83.

Feather, N. T. (1966). Effects of prior success and failure on expectations of success and subsequent performance. *Journal of Personality and Social Psychology, 3*, 287–298.

Feather, N. T. (1968). Change in confidence following success or failure as a predictor of subsequent performance. *Journal of Personality and Social Psychology, 13*, 129–144.

Felson, R. B. (1993). The (somewhat) social self: How others affect self-appraisals. (In J. Suls (Ed.), *The self in social perspective* (Vol. 4, pp. 1–26). Hillsdale, NJ: Erlbaum.)

Gabriel, M. T., Critelli, J. W., & Ee, J. S. (1994). Narcissistic illusions in self-evaluations of intelligence and attractiveness. *Journal of Personality, 62*, 143–155.

Huguet, P., Charbonnier, E., & Monteil, J. (1999). Productivity loss in performance groups: People who see themselves as average do not engage in social loafing. *Group Dynamics: Theory, Research, and Practice, 3*, 118–131.

John, O. P., & Robins, R. W. (1994). Accuracy and bias in self-perception: Individual differences in self-enhancement and the role of narcissism. *Journal of Personality and Social Psychology, 66*, 206–219.

Karau, S. J., & Williams, K. D. (1993). Social loafing: A meta-analytic review and theoretical integration. *Journal of Personality and Social Psychology, 65*, 681–706.

Kukla, A. (1972). Foundations of an attributional theory of performance. *Psychological Review, 79*, 454–470.

Kukla, A. (1974). Performance as a function of resultant achievement motivation (perceived ability) and perceived difficulty. *Journal of Research in Personality, 7*, 374–383.

Latane, B., Williams, K., & Harkins, S. (1979). Many hands make light the work: The causes and consequences of social loafing. *Journal of Personality and Social Psychology, 37*, 822–832.

Meyer, W. U. (1987). Perceived ability and achievement related behavior. (In F. Halisch & J. Kuhl (Eds.), *Motivation, intention, and volition* (pp. 73–86). Berlin, Germany: Springer-Verlag.)

Morf, C. C., & Rhodewalt, F. (2001). Unraveling the paradoxes of narcissism: A dynamic self-regulatory processing model. *Psychological Inquiry, 12*, 177–196.

Pajares, F. (1997). Current directions in self-efficacy research. (In M. L. Maehr & P. R. Pintrich (Eds.), *Advances in motivation and achievement* (Vol. 10, pp. 1–49). Greenwich, CT: JAI Press.)

Paulhus, D. L. (1998). Interpersonal and intrapsychic adaptiveness of trait self-enhancement: A mixed blessing? *Journal of Personality and Social Psychology, 74*, 1197–1208.

Raskin, R. N. (1980). Narcissism and creativity: Are they related? *Psychological Reports, 46*, 55–60.

Raskin, R. N., & Hall, C. S. (1979). A narcissistic personality inventory. *Psychological Reports, 45*, 590

Raskin, R., Novacek, J., & Hogan, R. (1991a). Narcissism, self-esteem, and defensive self-enhancement. *Journal of Personality, 59*, 19–38.

Raskin, R., & Terry, H. (1988). A principle-components analysis of the Narcissistic Personality Inventory and further evidence of its construct validity. *Journal of Personality and Social Psychology, 54*, 890–902.

Robins, R. W., & Beer, J. S. (2001). Positive illusions about the self: Short-term benefits and long-term costs. *Journal of Personality and Social Psychology, 80*, 340–352.

Robins, R. W., & John, O. P. (1997). Effects of visual perspective and narcissism on self-perception: Is seeing believing? *Psychological Science, 8*, 37–42.

Sanna, L. J. (1992). Self-efficacy theory: Implications for social facilitation and social loafing. *Journal of Personality and Social Psychology, 62*, 774–786.

Trope, Y. (1979). Uncertainty-reducing properties of achievement tasks. *Journal of Personality and Social Psychology, 37*, 1505–1518.

Tuckman, B. W., & Sexton, T. L. (1992). Self-believers are self-motivated; self-doubters are not. *Personality and Individual Differences, 13*, 425–428.

Watson, P. J., Sawrie, S. M., & Biderman, M. D. (1991). Personal control, assumptive worlds, and narcissism. *Journal of Social Behavior and Personality, 6*, 929–941.

Williams, K., Harkins, S., & Latane, B. (1981). Identifiability as a deterrent to social loafing: Two cheering experiments. *Journal of Personality and Social Psychology, 40*, 303–311.

Note: This research was part of Harry M. Wallace's doctoral dissertation, completed under the supervision of Roy F. Baumeister. Portions of this research were presented at the meetings of the Society for Personality and Social Psychology, February 2000, 2001, and 2002, Nashville, Tennessee, San Antonio, Texas, and Savannah, Georgia, respectively, and at the meeting of the American Psychological Society, June 2000, Miami Beach, Florida. We thank Kimberly Charlton, Elizabeth Fink, Kara Hultin, and Heather McGinness for helping to conduct these studies. We thank Kate Catanese, Natalie Ciarocco, Julie Exline, Jon Faber, Dave Kolb, and Dianne Tice for their comments on drafts of this article and Jean Twenge and Kathleen Vohs for their statistical advice. We especially thank Keith Campbell for his valuable insights and statistical guidance.

Address correspondence to: Harry M. Wallace, Department of Psychology, University of Florida, Gainesville, Florida, 32611-2250. Electronic mail may be sent to hwallace@ufl.edu

Discussion Questions for
Model Literature Review 1

Editorial note: All the sample literature reviews in this book are presented as strong models. However, there are differences of opinion on the effectiveness of any particular piece of writing, even among experts. While answering the following questions, consider the guidelines in this book (as *only* guidelines, not principles) as well as your own standards for effective writing.

1. Briefly comment on the adequacy of the title of the review. Note that this review was written as the introduction to a report on original research, which is not reprinted in this book. Hence, the title for this review refers largely to the findings of the authors' research. If this were a stand-alone review, do you think that the current title would be a good one? Explain.

2. Does the review have a strong beginning? Does it get straight to the point? If not, have the authors used some other effective technique to begin the review?

3. Have the authors made a strong case for reviewing the topic(s) they cover? Have they shown that the topic(s) are important?

4. Is the material presented in a logical sequence? Are the headings (and subheadings, if any) appropriate and helpful?

5. Are key variables adequately defined? Are they defined at appropriate points? Explain.

6. Are there points where the references are not well integrated with each other (i.e., simply described as an annotated list)? Explain.

7. Are the strengths and weaknesses of some of the cited research described? If yes, name at least one section where this is done using paragraph numbers.

8. Have the authors made it clear what material is theirs and what is being summarized/paraphrased from other sources? Explain.

9. Are any portions of the review unclear to you? If so, identify them by paragraph number(s).

10. Are the individual paragraphs straightforward and to the point? Explain. If yes, identify one by number that you think is especially good. If no, identify one that is weak.

11. Is the conclusion/discussion at the end of the review appropriate in light of the material covered earlier?

12. On a scale from 1 (very weak) to 10 (very strong), what is your overall evaluation of the literature review? Name one or two considerations that strongly influenced your evaluation.

13. Assume that you are on the editorial board of an academic journal and that the general topic of this review is within the scope of what the journal usually publishes. Which of the following would you recommend to the editor of the journal: publish as is, publish only after minor revisions, publish only after major revisions, *or* do not publish? Briefly defend your recommendation.

Model Literature Review 2

The Inherent Limits of Predicting School Violence

Edward P. Mulvey
University of Pittsburgh

Elizabeth Cauffman
University of Pittsburgh

Editorial note: The paragraphs in this literature review have been numbered to make it easy to refer to specific portions of this review during classroom discussions. The numbers are italicized superscripts, which appear at the beginning of each paragraph. All other superscripts, if any, refer to footnotes within the review.

ABSTRACT

The recent media hype over school shootings has led to demands for methods of identifying school shooters before they act. Despite the fact that schools remain one of the safest places for youths to be, schools are beginning to adopt identification systems to determine which students could be future killers. The methods used to accomplish this not only are unproven but are inherently limited in usefulness and often do more harm than good for both the children and the school setting. The authors' goals in the present article are to place school shootings in perspective relative to other risks of violence that children face and to provide a reasonable and scientifically defensible approach to improving the safety of schools.

[1]School violence, having been dubbed a crisis, permeates the national consciousness and media outlets. This concern, moreover, has gone beyond simple statements and speculations. A heightened awareness of the potential tragedy of a school-related violent incident has prompted school administrators, law enforcement professionals, and mental health professionals to put into place methods for identifying and intervening proactively with potentially violent students and situations. Many communities have seen curriculum changes, the adoption of "safe school" policies, new weapons-reporting requirements, and increased efforts to refer problem students to mental health professionals. For example, several years ago, New York City spent over $28 million dollars on metal detectors (Kemper, 1993), and numerous school districts have implemented mandatory school uniform policies to cut down on gang identification (Stephens, 1998). After the shooting at Columbine High School, the principal distributed a memorandum requesting students to report on other students whom they deemed to be demonstrating maladaptive behavior (e.g., dressing oddly, being loners; Aronson, 2000). Currently, professionals seem open to trying just about anything to combat the perceived dangers of school violence.

[2]In the midst of these activities, it is important to note that such policy changes are fueled primarily by graphic images of children killing and being killed at school rather than by actual numbers indicating an epidemic of violence. Data from the National Crime Victimization Survey and the School Crime Supplement, for example, suggest that there is virtually no difference between the rates of criminal victimization in schools in 1989 and the rates of victimization in 1995 (Snyder & Sickmund, 1999). Other examinations of the figures regarding adolescent deaths indicate that violent deaths are a rare event, with less than 1% of the homicides and suicides among school-age children occurring in or around school grounds (Kachur et al., 1996). Moreover, the rate of violent crimes committed by juveniles remains low during the school day, but it spikes at the close of the school day and declines throughout the evening hours (Snyder & Sickmund, 1999), indicating that school hours are probably the safest time of the day for adolescents.

[3]Yet, somehow, the images of the violence at Columbine, Padukah, and Santee are more persistent than the realities of the situations connected with the 99% of school-age victims who meet their fate when school is not in session. That students are very unlikely to be assaulted in the school setting and that urban adolescents are safer in their schools than on their way to or from school do not emerge as key points in most discussions of school violence. As Joseph Stalin, of all people, noted in another time, "A single death is a tragedy, a million deaths is a statistic" (as quoted in Bartlett, 1980, p. 766).

Unfortunately, there now may have been enough tragedies to precipitate action.

[4]An attractive strategy for addressing school violence is to increase efforts at early detection of and intervention with adolescents who are likely to commit these horrible acts. One of the most common reactions to the adolescents who opened fire in Padukah, Columbine, or Santee is to ask, "How could someone not have known that this adolescent was in trouble?" The problem, of course, is that it is not often clear exactly what to look for, who should have looked for it, or what should have been done if someone had seen something. Indeed, in postmortems of these situations, one often picks up signs of distress or despair in these adolescents, but one is rarely sure if the level or types of indicators found would have been enough to make even a vigilant and caring adult do something markedly different than what was done. After all, for every killer youth, there are many others with the same behaviors or attitudes who never come close to killing their classmates.

[5]The inability to see clear markers of trouble in these cases should reveal something. It should make clear the daunting nature of the identification task taken on by many school administrators and mental health professionals. Identification of adolescents who are at high risk for committing serious, public acts of violence poses many inherent challenges; considering these can lead psychologists to think more realistically about where to direct their energies for interventions for school violence.

The Characteristics of Adolescent Violence and the Identification Process

[6]The first challenge facing any system for identifying adolescents who could commit serious acts of violence in school is that the behavior being predicted is a rare event. There are severe restrictions on the ability of any predictive strategy (even if reasonably accurate) to identify true positives for a low base-rate behavior without also identifying a large number of false positives (Hart, Webster, & Menzies, 1993; Meehl, 1954). Identification of large numbers of false positives is not a problem if such identification causes no harm (Morris & Miller, 1985), but the ratio of true positives to false positives matters greatly if all identified individuals are stigmatized or if their opportunities are limited. One way to avoid the low base-rate problem is to expand the definition of the violent outcome being predicted, effectively converting many false positives into true positives. If one includes bullying, threats, and fistfights in the definition of school violence, the base rate increases dra

matically, and the ability to predict who might be involved in these activities may increase. According to the Centers for Disease Control and Prevention's 1997 Youth Risk Behavior Surveillance System, 37% of high school students said they had been in a physical fight during the past school year (Centers for Disease Control and Prevention, 1997); approximately 80% of youths have indicated that they engage in some form of bullying behavior such as pushing, teasing, or threatening others (Bosworth, Espelage, & Simon, 1999). With this expanded definition, however, comes a blurring of the behavior being examined and a good chance that the processes behind these behaviors will become more heterogeneous. Taken to extremes, this approach amounts to dealing with a problem that is hard to solve by choosing to solve a different problem. If the identified problems are too broadly defined, the intervention strategy is reduced to meeting the needs of the general pool of troubled adolescents found in any school, and the hard-to-solve problem of identifying potentially violent adolescents is dealt with by choosing to solve the problem of disruptive students.

[7]The second major obstacle to identifying students who are likely to be involved in serious school violence is that the event being predicted is usually embedded in a social and transactional sequence of events. One thing that is clear about youth violence in general and seemingly about many of the recent tragedies is that this behavior has a heavy social component (Staub & Rosenthal, 1994). Youths who engage in criminal behavior, both violent and nonviolent, are not usually loners. For example, 60% of juvenile offenders who committed assault were with peers at the time, and 90% of juvenile offenders who committed robbery were with adolescent peers (Zimring, 1981, 1998). Moreover, youths who are aggressive not only seek each other out but also form coercive cliques (Cairns, Cairns, Neckerman, Gest, & Gariepy, 1988; Coie & Dodge, 1998), which in turn provide a training ground for subsequent delinquent behaviors (Parker & Asher, 1987; Patterson, Reid, & Dishion, 1992). Predictably, then, it appears that for both lethal and nonlethal incidents, school violence is more likely to occur in larger rather than smaller schools and in "unowned" areas such as hallways, dining areas, and parking lots (Astor, Meyer, & Behre, 1999). Furthermore, violent events in the schools are part of a chain of actions and reactions, often among numerous other individuals (e.g., taunting peers, disinterested girlfriends or boyfriends, uninterested parents; see Fagan & Wilkinson, 1998), and bystanders appear to be a critical component of the escalation of disputes into violence

(Decker, 1996; Tedeschi & Felson, 1994). Previous research has shown that these events do not occur in a vacuum and that there are numerous rationales for and pathways to the violent act. Identification based only on the characteristics of an individual neglects these highly salient social and transactional aspects of school violence.

[8]The third major obstacle to the task of identification is that the individuals being assessed are adolescents whose characters are often not yet fully formed. Research in the areas of physical development (Buchanan, Eccles, & Becker, 1992), psychosocial development (Cauffman & Steinberg, 2000; Steinberg & Cauffman, 1996), and even brain development (Baird et al., 1999; Giedd et al., 1999; Sowell, Thompson, Holmes, Jernigan, & Toga, 1999) suggests that adolescents are still changing and that their characters are not yet fully formed. Assessing adolescents, therefore, presents the formidable challenge of trying to capture a rapidly changing process with few trustworthy markers. Diagnostic systems for adolescents are not as well developed as those for adult disorders, many disorders do not emerge clearly until young adulthood, and the diagnostic tools used to assess adults are often of questionable value when applied to adolescents. Despite these limitations, adult diagnoses or concepts periodically have been applied to children, adolescents, or both without taking into account important developmental factors that may affect the applicability or validity of these constructs (for a review, see Achenbach, 1995). For example, some characteristics that are viewed as risk factors for psychopathy among adults (e.g., impulsivity, little concern for future consequences) are common and transitory aspects of normal adolescent development and may be easily misinterpreted when using standard approaches (Edens, Skeem, Cruise, & Cauffman, 2001). These realities make assessments of adolescents by mental health professionals using tools designed for adults difficult to interpret meaningfully.

[9]Finally, it is not clear what interventions are likely to work with violence-prone adolescents. Part of the reason for identifying an adolescent who is at high risk for serious violence is to prevent the occurrence of an incident. This can be done either by imposing restrictions on the adolescent (e.g., enforcing some schedule or activity restrictions) or by altering the processes within the adolescent or in his or her life that might be contributing to the violence (e.g., enrolling the adolescent in an anger-management group). Unfortunately, most of the single-focus interventions for violent adolescents have demonstrated limited effectiveness (McCord, Widom, &

Crowell, 2001; U.S. Department of Health and Human Services, 2001), and the most successful interventions with antisocial adolescents work in multiple community settings and focus on building specific skills (Lipsey & Wilson, 1998). Schools can certainly provide valuable prevention programs, such as social skills training, but these settings are not generally well equipped to deliver individualized, broadly based services to small numbers of identified students.

Recasting the Problem as Risk Management

[10]This dismal picture does not justify inaction. The limits of identification and intervention are real and substantial, but they should be used to inform people about reasonable strategies rather than discourage them from facing the problem. They highlight the need for professionals to take a realistic view of what might be accomplished through the development of early identification systems and to focus planning and programming in a way that increases the likelihood of success.

[11]Perhaps the first step is to approach the problem as one of ongoing risk assessment rather than prediction. A great deal can be learned in this regard from the progress that has been made over the past 20 years regarding management of violence in mentally ill adults (see Borum, 1996; Otto, 1992). In this area, as in the area of school violence, the goal is to predict and prevent rare, socially embedded violence for which little effective intervention technology exists. Trends in preventing violence in mentally ill adults, however, have been moving away from framing the problem as one of predicting an event and toward the approach of managing risk (Heilbrun, 1997). Ongoing risk assessment and management have replaced prediction of dangerousness, a shift with subtle but important implications for policy, practice, and research (Skeem & Mulvey, in press).

[12]This new approach recognizes that violence risk is a dynamic, rather than static, process. Although it is possible to sort individuals into high- and low-risk groups generally, the task of managing risk effectively requires an ongoing evaluation of the factors that increase or decrease the likelihood of a violent incident in individuals at relatively high risk already (Monahan & Steadman, 1996; Mulvey & Lidz, 1998). A risk management approach thus starts out much like a more traditional predictive strategy by using available indicators of generalized risk for adolescents and some structured data-collection scheme to sort individuals into a high- or low-risk status. This identification process, however, is only the first step toward avoiding violent incidents. The

next step is to monitor the ongoing changes in the lives of these individuals for transitions or turning points that may further increase the likelihood of violence.

[13]Framing the problem in this way might well change the focus of school violence programs. Rather than developing more elaborate and potentially discriminatory or arbitrary approaches to choosing those who might be at highest risk, researchers could direct more resources into ongoing involvement with the group of individuals who are clearly high risk. The natural reaction in the face of disastrous violence in schools is to look for a system that can pick out the people who may react similarly in the future. The reality of prediction, however, is that this is a largely futile task. The fuzziness of the categories, the base rate of the behavior being predicted, and the timeframe to which the prediction applies must always compromise any identification scheme for schoolyard killers. Therefore, rather than being used to make a marginal improvement in a sorting algorithm to identify troubled students, resources may well be better spent monitoring the activities of those students who would be identified under just about any risk-assessment method.

Need for a Focus on School Environment

[14]Although easier to do than accurately modeling individual behavior using a violence-prediction machine, keeping abreast of the ongoing activities of troubled and troubling adolescents is no easy feat. Now, as always, the best source of information about the activities of students in a school is other students. A long line of research has demonstrated that students are well aware of the problem children in their own classrooms (for a review, see Hartup, 1992). For example, since the advent of sociometric research in 1934, researchers have been able to identify which youths are liked or disliked by their peers, as well as future delinquent behaviors among youths (Rubin, Bukowski, & Parker, 1998). Ignoring this potentially rich source of information in favor of structured psychological assessment places unwarranted faith in the powers of individual assessment. Peers and teachers who talk with problem students can often provide the most useful information about when such students are in trouble.

[15]For such information to flow from students to administrators requires an atmosphere where sharing in good faith is respected and honored. Giving information about the problems that another student is having or about threats or scary activities going on in a school environment can occur only if students feel that they are (and will remain) safe and that a reasoned response will

result from their reporting. Getting accurate information about the activities of high-risk students on an ongoing basis, therefore, rests heavily on establishing and maintaining a supportive school environment.

[16]Ironically, many schools appear to be taking the opposite approach. Instead of working to foster a sense of belonging, schools are implementing zero-tolerance policies that virtually guarantee an unreasoned response to any reported problem. For example, when a student is expelled or suspended for carrying aspirin (in violation of a zero-tolerance drug policy), that student is likely to hold the school administration in contempt. It is also likely that other students will withhold information from the administration to avoid such disproportionate punishments. This change in school atmosphere is all too real. For example, in a *New York Times* op-ed piece written by a high school student from Littleton, Colorado, the student remarked as follows:

> [17]High school students in Littleton now have a new excuse to get out of class for a few extra minutes: the lockdown drill.... Apart from the lockdown drills, there have been few changes in security procedures. The greatest change has been the increase of paranoia. For example, a few weeks after the shooting I was working on a graph assignment with a friend. We arranged the points on the graph to spell out a humorous but inappropriate message. A month earlier, my friend would have said, "The teacher's going to be mad." This time he said, "If we turn this in, we'll be expelled." There's the difference. (Black, 2001, p. A23)

[18]Empirical evidence, meanwhile, seems to support the contention that promoting healthy relationships and environments is more effective for reducing school misconduct and crime than instituting punitive penalties (Nettles, Mucherah, & Jones, 2000). For example, a study of 7th-, 8th-, and 9th-grade students found that commitment to school and belief in the fairness and consistent enforcement of school rules are the most important elements in reducing school crime (Jenkins, 1997). Similarly, the National Longitudinal Study of Adolescent Health found that among a nationally representative sample of 7th–12th graders, attachment to family and school served as protective factors against violence (Franke, 2000), a result consistent with earlier research indicating that adolescents with a low commitment to school are at increased risk of engaging in violent behavior (Cernkovich & Giordano, 1992; Farrington, 1991). Also, a study of school-based violence-prevention interventions found that between 1993 and 1997, elementary schools that focused on the broader school environment appeared successful in changing violence-related behavior (Howard, Flora, & Griffin,

1999). Finally, the most powerful predictor of adolescent well-being is a feeling of connection to school (Resnick et al., 1997), and students who feel close to others, fairly treated, and vested in school are less likely to engage in risky behaviors than those who do not (Resnick et al., 1997). Each of these studies suggests that a key factor in preventing school violence is students' positive relations to their school environments. Students who are committed to school, feel that they belong, and trust the administration are less likely to commit violent acts than those who are uninvolved, alienated, or distrustful.

Conclusion

[19]In sum, preventing violent incidents in school does not require either more sophisticated methods for assessing students individually or a magical, uniform method for intervening with them for a short while after they have been identified. It seems instead to rest largely on developing a positive and supportive organizational climate in a school. A crucial component of any school violence program is thus a school environment where ongoing activities and problems of students are discussed, rather than tallied with structured assessment instruments. Such an environment promotes ongoing risk management, which can be achieved only with the support and involvement of those closest to the indicators of trouble.

[20]It is also worth noting that school violence is rarely just about what happens in school. Gun-related violence outside the school is a better predictor of weapon-related victimization at or during travel to and from school than is the dangerousness of the school environment itself (Sheley, McGee, & Wright, 1995), and neighborhood conditions such as poverty, population turnover, and crime rates are the strongest predictors of school violence (Laub & Lauritsen, 1998). Community incidents are carried into the school environment, just as the effects of the school day's events linger on after dismissal.

[21]Although connecting schools with families and communities is often given as a mantra for school reform, it is worth chanting once more when discussing interventions to prevent school violence. The indicators of trouble for violence-prone adolescents can come from a variety of sources, and often, the only way one can obtain a clear picture of what is moving an adolescent toward violence is by looking at the adolescent's world from the broadest perspective. Strategies designed to address school violence must recognize the interdependence of school violence with neighborhood and family conditions.

[22]This call for an emphasis on organizational issues for the prevention of school violence reflects a recognition that there will never be a technology that matches the desire to find and control the uncontrollable events of life. Violence of the sort seen recently in schools is horrific and compels society to reestablish order in the face of chaos. Unfortunately, the technology of predicting rare events will always be a poor substitute for solid human relations and sound organizational management. Establishing school environments where students feel connected and trusted will build the critical link between those who often know when trouble is brewing and those who can act to prevent it.

References

Achenbach, T. M. (1995). Developmental issues in assessment, taxonomy, and diagnosis of child and adolescent psychopathology. In D. Cicchetti & D. J. Cohen (Eds.), *Developmental psychopathology, Vol. 1: Theory and methods* (pp. 57–80). New York: Wiley.

Aronson, E. (2000). *Nobody left to hate: Teach compassion after Columbine.* New York: Worth.

Astor, R., Meyer, H., & Behre, W. (1999). Unowned places and times: Maps and interviews about violence in high schools. *American Educational Research Journal, 36,* 3–42.

Baird, A., Gruber, S., Fein, D., Maas, L., Steingard, R., Renshaw, P., Cohen, B., & Yurgelun-Todd, D. (1999). Functional magnetic resonance imaging of facial affect recognition in children and adolescents. *Journal of the American Academy of Child and Adolescent Psychiatry, 38,* 195–199.

Bartlett, J. (1980). *Bartlett's familiar quotations* (15th ed.). Boston: Little, Brown.

Black, N. (2001, March 8). After a shooting. *The New York Times,* p. A23.

Borum, R. (1996). Improving the clinical practice of violence risk assessment: Technology, guidelines, and training. *American Psychologist, 51,* 945–948.

Bosworth, K., Espelage, D., & Simon, T. (1999). Factors associated with bullying behavior in middle school students. *Journal of Early Adolescence, 19,* 341–362.

Buchanan, C. M., Eccles, J. S., & Becker, J. B. (1992). Are adolescents victims of raging hormones? Evidence for activational effects of hormones on moods and behavior at adolescence. *Psychological Bulletin, 111,* 62–107.

Cairns, R., Cairns, B., Neckerman, H., Gest, S., & Gariepy, J. (1988). Social networks and aggressive behavior: Peer support or peer rejection? *Developmental Psychology, 24,* 815–823.

Cauffman, E., & Steinberg, L. (2000). (Im)maturity of judgment in adolescence: Why adolescents may be less culpable than adults. *Behavioral Sciences and the Law, 18,* 741–760.

Centers for Disease Control and Prevention. (1997). Rates of homicide, suicide, and firearm-related death among children—26 industrialized countries. *Morbidity and Mortality Weekly Report, 46,* 101–105.

Cernkovich, S. A., & Giordano, P. C. (1992). School bonding, race, and delinquency. *Criminology, 31,* 261–291.

Coie, J., & Dodge, K. (1998). Aggression and antisocial behavior. In W. Damon & N. Eisenberg (Eds.), *Handbook of child psychology* (pp. 779–862). New York: Wiley.

Decker, S. (1996). Reconstructing homicide events: The role of witnesses in fatal encounters. *Journal of Criminal Justice, 23,* 439–450.

Edens, J., Skeem, J., Cruise, K., & Cauffman, E. (2001). The assessment of juvenile psychopathy and its association with violence: A critical review. *Behavioral Sciences and the Law, 19,* 53–80.

Fagan, J., & Wilkinson, D. (1998). Social contexts and functions of adolescent violence. In D. Elliott, B. Hamburg, & K. Williams (Eds.), *Violence in American schools* (pp. 55–93). New York: Cambridge University Press.

Farrington, D. (1991). Childhood aggression and adult violence: Early precursors and later life outcomes. In D. Pepper & K. Rubin (Eds.), *The development and treatment of childhood aggression* (pp. 5–29). Hillsdale, NJ: Erlbaum.

Franke, T. (2000). The role of attachment as a protective factor in adolescent violent behavior. *Adolescent and Family Health, 1,* 40–51.

Giedd, J., Blumenthal, J., Jeffries, N., Castellanos, F., Liu, H., Zijdenbos, A., Paus, T., Evans, A., & Rapoport, J. (1999). Brain development during childhood and adolescence: A longitudinal MRI study. *Nature Neuroscience, 2,* 861–863.

Hart, S. D., Webster, C. D. & Menzies, R. J. (1993). A note on portraying the accuracy of violence predictions. *Law and Human Behavior, 17,* 695–700.

Hartup, W. (1992). Peer relations in early and middle childhood. In V. B. Van Hasselt & M. Hersen (Eds.), *Handbook of social development: A lifespan perspective* (pp. 257–281). New York: Plenum.

Heilbrun, K. (1997). Prediction versus management models relevant to risk assessment: The importance of legal decision-making context. *Law and Human Behavior, 21,* 347–359.

Howard, K., Flora, J., & Griffin, M. (1999). Violence-prevention programs in schools: State of the science and implications for future research. *Applied and Preventive Psychology, 8,* 197–215.

Jenkins, P. (1997). School delinquency and the school social bond. *Journal of Research in Crime and Delinquency, 34,* 337–367.

Kachur, S. P., Stennies, G., Powell, K., Modzeleski, W., Stephens, R., Murphy, R., Kresnow, M., Sleet, D., & Lowry, R. (1996). School-associated deaths in the United States, 1992–1994. *JAMA, 275,* 1729–1733.

Kemper, P. (1993, Fall). Disarming youth. *California School Boards Journal, 25*–33.

Laub, J., & Lauritsen, J. (1998). The interdependence of school violence with neighborhood and family conditions. In D. Elliott, B. Hamburg, & K. Williams (Eds.), *Violence in American schools* (pp. 55–93). New York: Cambridge University Press.

Lipsey, M., & Wilson, D. (1998). Effective intervention for serious juvenile offenders: A synthesis of research. In R. Loeber & D. Farrington (Eds.), *Serious and violent juvenile offenders: Risk factors and successful interventions* (pp. 313–345). Thousand Oaks, CA: Sage.

McCord, J., Widom, C. S., & Crowell, N. A. (Eds.) (2001). *Juvenile crime, juvenile justice.* Washington, DC: National Academy Press.

Meehl, P. E. (1954). *Clinical versus statistical prediction: A theoretical analysis and a review of the evidence.* Minneapolis: University of Minnesota Press.

Monahan, J., & Steadman, H. (1996). Violent storms and violent people: How meteorology can inform risk communication in mental health law. *American Psychologist, 51,* 931–938.

Morris, N., & Miller, M. (1985). Predictions of dangerousness. In M. Tonry & N. Morris (Eds.), *Crime and justice: An annual review of research* (Vol. 6, pp. 1–50). Chicago: University of Chicago Press.

Mulvey, E. P., & Lidz, C. W. (1998). The clinical prediction of violence as a conditional judgment. *Social Psychiatry and Psychiatric Epidemiology, 33,* 107–113.

Nettles, S., Mucherah, W., & Jones, D. (2000). Understanding resilience: The role of social resources. *Journal of Education for Students Placed at Risk, 5,* 47–60.

Otto, R. K. (1992). Prediction of dangerous behavior: A review and analysis of "second-generation" research. *Forensic Reports, 5,* 103–133.

Parker, J., & Asher, S. (1987). Peer relations and later personal adjustment: Are low-accepted children at risk? *Psychological Bulletin, 102,* 357–389.

Patterson, G., Reid, J., & Dishion, T. (1992). *Antisocial boys.* Eugene, OR: Castalia.

Resnick, M., Bearman, P., Blum, R., Bauman, K., Harris, K., Jones, J., Tabor, J., Beuhring, T., Sieving, R., Shew, M., Ireland, M., Bearinger, L., & Udry, R. (1997). Protecting adolescents from harm: Findings from the National Longitudinal Study on Adolescent Health. *JAMA, 278,* 823–832.

Rubin, K., Bukowski, W., & Parker, J. (1998). Peer interactions, relationships, and groups. In W. Damon & N. Eisenberg (Eds.), *Handbook of child psychology* (pp. 619–700). New York: Wiley.

Sheley, J., McGee, Z., & Wright, J. (1995). Gun-related violence in and around inner-city schools. *American Journal of Diseases of Children, 146,* 677–682.

Skeem, J., & Mulvey, E. (in press). Assessing the violence potential of mentally disordered offenders being treated in the community. In A. Buchanan (Ed.), *Care of the mentally disordered offender in the community.* Oxford, England: Oxford University Press.

Snyder, H., & Sickmund, M. (1999). *Juvenile offenders and victims: 1999 national report.* Washington, DC: Office of Juvenile Justice and Delinquency Prevention.

Sowell, E., Thompson, P., Holmes, C., Jernigan, T., & Toga, A. (1999). In vivo evidence for post-adolescent brain maturation in frontal and striatal regions. *Nature Neuroscience, 2,* 859–861.

Staub, E., & Rosenthal, L. (1994). Mob violence: Cultural—societal sources, instigators, group processes, and participants. In L. Eron & J. Gentry (Eds.), *Reason to hope: A psychosocial perspective on violence and youth* (pp. 281–313). Washington, DC: American Psychological Association.

Steinberg, L., & Cauffman, E. (1996). Maturity of judgment in adolescence: Psychosocial factors in adolescent decision making. *Law and Human Behavior, 20,* 249–272.

Stephens, R. (1998). Safe school planning. In D. Elliott, B. Hamburg, & K. Williams (Eds.), *Violence in American schools* (pp. 253–289). New York: Cambridge University Press.

Tedeschi, J., & Felson, R. (1994). *Violence, aggression, and coercive actions.* Washington, DC: American Psychological Association.

U.S. Department of Health and Human Services. (2001). *Youth violence: A report of the Surgeon General.* Washington, DC: Author.

Zimring, F. (1981). Kids, groups, and crime: Some implications of a well-known secret. *Journal of Criminal Law and Criminology, 72,* 867.

Zimring, F. (1998). *American youth violence.* New York: Oxford University Press.

Address correspondence to: Edward P. Mulvey, Law and Psychiatry Program, Western Psychiatric Institute and Clinic, University of Pittsburgh, 3811 O'Hara Street, Pittsburgh, PA 15213. E-mail: mulveyep@msx.upmc.edu

From *American Psychologist, 56,* 797–802. Copyright © 2001 by the American Psychological Association. Reprinted with permission.

Discussion Questions for
Model Literature Review 2

Editorial note: All the sample literature reviews in this book are presented as strong models. However, there are differences of opinion on the effectiveness of any particular piece of writing, even among experts. While answering the following questions, consider the guidelines in this book (as *only* guidelines, not principles) as well as your own standards for effective writing.

1. Briefly comment on the adequacy of the title of the review.

2. Comment on the adequacy of the Abstract. Does it effectively summarize the essence of the review given that abstracts are restricted to 120 words or less in the journal in which this review article appeared?

3. Does the review have a strong beginning? Does it get straight to the point? If not, have the authors used some other effective technique to begin the review?

4. Have the authors made a strong case for reviewing the topic(s) they cover? Have they shown that the topic(s) are important?

5. Is the material presented in a logical sequence? Are the headings (and subheadings, if any) appropriate and helpful?

6. Are key variables adequately defined? Are they defined at appropriate points? Explain.

7. Are there points where the references are not well integrated with each other (i.e., simply described as an annotated list)? Explain.

8. Are the strengths and weaknesses of some of the cited research described? If yes, name at least one section where this is done using paragraph numbers.

9. Have the authors made it clear what material is theirs and what is being summarized/paraphrased from other sources? Explain.

10. Are any portions of the review unclear to you? If so, identify them by paragraph number(s).

11. Are the individual paragraphs straightforward and to the point? Explain. If yes, identify one by number that you think is especially good. If no, identify one that is weak.

12. Is the conclusion/discussion at the end of the review appropriate in light of the material covered earlier?

13. On a scale from 1 (very weak) to 10 (very strong), what is your overall evaluation of the literature review? Name one or two considerations that strongly influenced your evaluation.

14. Assume that you are on the editorial board of an academic journal and that the general topic of this review is within the scope of what the journal usually publishes. Which of the following would you recommend to the editor of the journal: publish as is, publish only after minor revisions, publish only after major revisions, *or* do not publish? Briefly defend your recommendation.

Model Literature Review 3

Research on Religion-Accommodative Counseling: Review and Meta-Analysis

Michael E. McCullough
National Institute for Healthcare Research

Editorial note: The paragraphs in this literature review have been numbered to make it easy to refer to specific portions of this review during classroom discussions. The numbers are italicized superscripts, which appear at the beginning of each paragraph. All other superscripts, if any, refer to footnotes within the review.

ABSTRACT

The present meta-analysis examined data from 5 studies ($N = 111$) that compared the efficacy of standard approaches to counseling for depression with religion-accommodative approaches. There was no evidence that the religion-accommodative approaches were more or less efficacious than the standard approaches. Findings suggest that the choice to use religious approaches with religious clients is probably more a matter of client preference than a matter of differential efficacy. However, additional research is needed to examine whether religion-accommodative approaches yield differential treatment satisfaction or differential improvements in spiritual well-being or facilitate relapse prevention. Given the importance of religion to many potential consumers of psychological services, counseling psychologists should devote greater attention to religion-accommodative counseling in future studies.

[1]The United States is a highly religious country; 92% of its population are affiliated with a religion (Kosmin & Lachman, 1993). According to a 1995 survey, 96% of Americans believe in God or a universal spirit, 42% indicate that they attend a religious worship service weekly or almost weekly, 67% indicate that they are members of a church or synagogue, and 60% indicate that religion is "important" or "very important" in their lives (Gallup, 1995).

[2]In addition, many scholars acknowledge that certain forms of religious involvement are associated with better functioning on a variety of measures of mental health. Reviews of this research (e.g., Bergin, 1991; Bergin, Masters, & Richards, 1987; Larson et al., 1992; Pargament, 1997; Schumaker, 1992; Worthington, Kurusu, McCullough, & Sandage, 1996) suggested that several forms of religious involvement (including intrinsic religious motivation, attendance at religious worship, receiving coping support from one's religious faith or religious congregation, and positive religious attributions for life events) are positively associated with a variety of measures of mental health. For example, various measures of religious involvement appear to be related to lower degrees of depressive symptoms in adults (Bienenfeld, Koenig, Larson, & Sherrill, 1997; Ellison, 1995; Kendler, Gardner, & Prescott, 1997) and children (Miller, Warner, Wickramaratne, & Weissman, 1997) and less suicide (e.g., Comstock & Partridge, 1972; Kark et al., 1996; Wandrei, 1985).

[3]Koenig, George, and Peterson (1998) reported that depressed people scoring high on measures of intrinsic religiousness were significantly more likely to experience a remission of depression during nearly a 1-year follow-up than were depressed people with lower intrinsic religiousness, even after controlling for 30 potential demographic, psychosocial, and medical confounds. Other studies have shown that religious involvement, as gauged through single-item measures of frequency of religious worship and private prayer as well as more complex measures of religious coping, is related to positive psychological outcomes after major life events (e.g., Pargament et al., 1990; Pargament et al., 1994; Pargament, Smith, & Brant, 1995). This is the case even though several patterns of religious belief and religious coping (e.g., the belief that one's misfortunes are a punishment from God) are associated with greater psychological distress (Pargament, 1997).

Religion in Counseling and Psychotherapy

[4]Some scholars (e.g., Bergin, 1991; Payne, Bergin,

Table 1

Sample Sizes, Effect Sizes, and 95% Confidence Intervals (CI) for the Studies Included in the Meta-Analysis

Study	Religion-accommodative treatment n	Standard treatment n	Effect size (d_+)	95% CI
Propst (1980)	7	10	+0.41	−0.56/+1.39
Pecheur & Edwards (1984)	7	7	+0.53	−0.53/+1.60
Propst et al. (1992)	19	19	+0.51	−0.14/+1.15
W. B. Johnson & Ridley (1992a)	5	5	+0.29	−0.96/+1.53
W. B. Johnson et al. (1994)	16	16	−0.51	−1.22/+0.19

& Loftus, 1992; Richards & Bergin, 1997; Shafranske, 1996; Worthington et al., 1996) posited that considering clients' religiousness while designing treatment plans might have an important effect on the efficacy of treatment. Surveys of psychiatrists (Neeleman & King, 1993), psychologists (Bergin & Jensen, 1988; Shafranske & Malony, 1990), and mental health counselors (Kelly, 1995) also indicate that many mental health professionals believe that religious and spiritual values can and should be thoughtfully addressed in the course of mental health treatment. Moreover, a variety of analogue and clinical studies (e.g., Houts & Graham, 1986; T. A. Kelly & Strupp, 1992; Lewis & Lewis, 1985; McCullough & Worthington, 1995; McCullough, Worthington, Maxey, & Rachal, 1997; Morrow, Worthington, & McCullough, 1993) indicate that clients' religious beliefs can influence both (a) the conclusions of clinicians' structured psychological assessments and (b) the process of psychotherapy (cf. Luborsky et al., 1980).

Evidence from Comparative Efficacy Studies

[5]Given the existing research on religion and mental health, an important question for counseling psychologists is whether supporting clients' religious beliefs and values in a structured treatment package yield clinical benefits that are equal to or greater than standard methods of psychological practice. Several empirical studies have addressed this issue. Although the findings of studies that have examined such questions have been reviewed in narrative fashion elsewhere (e.g., W. B. Johnson, 1993; Matthews et al., 1998; Worthington et al., 1996), no researchers have used meta-analytic methods to estimate quantitatively the differential efficacy of such treatments. Meta-analytic reviews that compare religious approaches to counseling with standard approaches to counseling are one of three meta-analytic strategies that can be used to examine whether a given therapeutic approach has therapeutic efficacy (Wampold, 1997).

[6]In the present article, I review the existing research on such religious approaches to counseling using quantitative methods of research synthesis (e.g., Cooper & Hedges, 1994; Hunter & Schmidt, 1990) to estimate the differential efficacy of religious approaches in comparison to standard forms of counseling for depressed religious clients.

Method

Literature Search

[7]The PsycLIT, PsycINFO, Medline, ERIC, and Dissertation Abstracts electronic databases were searched through August 1998 for published and unpublished studies that examined the differential efficacy of a religion-accommodative approach to counseling in comparison to a standard approach to counseling. The reference sections of relevant articles were searched for other studies that would be relevant to this review. This search process continued until no new studies were revealed. In addition, several experts in the field of religion and mental health were contacted to identify unpublished studies.

[8]Studies had to meet four criteria to be included in the meta-analytic sample: They had to (a) compare a religion-accommodative approach to counseling to a standard approach to counseling; (b) randomly assign patients to treatments; (c) involve patients who were suffering from a specific set of psychological symptoms (e.g., anxiety or depression); and (d) offer equal amounts of treatment to clients in the religion-accommodative and standard treatments. Five published studies and one unpublished dissertation (W. B. Johnson, 1991), which was later reported in W. B. Johnson, DeVries, Ridley, Pettorini, and Peterson (1994) met these inclusion criteria. Several studies that investigated religious approaches to psychological treatment (e.g., Azhar & Varma, 1995a, 1995b; Azhar, Varma, & Dharap, 1994; Carlson, Bacaseta, & Simanton, 1988; Richards, Owen, & Stein, 1993; Rye & Pargament, 1997; Toh & Tan, 1997) were obtained, but these studies failed to meet all four inclusion criteria. Thus, they were omitted from the

meta-analytic sample. A single rater determined which studies met inclusion criteria. This rater's decisions were made without reference to the results or discussion sections of the articles.

[9]The resulting meta-analytic sample included five studies representing data from 111 counseling clients. Descriptions of study populations, measures used, and effect size estimates (with 95% confidence intervals) are given in Table 1.

The Studies

[10]Researchers interested in accommodative forms of religious counseling have taken standard cognitive–behavioral protocols or specific techniques, such as cognitive restructuring (Beck, Rush, Shaw, & Emery, 1979), cognitive coping skills (Meichenbaum, 1985), and appeals to rational thinking (e.g., Ellis & Grieger, 1977), and have developed religion-friendly rationales for and versions of such protocols or techniques (W. B. Johnson & Ridley, 1992b). These adapted protocols or techniques are thought to be theoretically equivalent to standard cognitive–behavioral techniques (Propst, 1996), but more amenable to the religious world view and religious language that religious clients use to understand their lives and their problems. The five studies are described in greater detail next.

[11]*Propst (1980).* Propst (1980) examined the differential efficacy of a manualized, religion-accommodative approach to cognitive restructuring and imagery modification. Volunteers who scored in the mild or moderate range of depression on the Beck Depression Inventory (BDI; Beck, Ward, Mendelson, Mock, & Erbaugh, 1961) and in at least the moderate range on the King and Hunt (1972) religion scales were randomly assigned to one of two treatments. The standard treatment was an integration of Beck's (1976) cognitive therapy for depression and Meichenbaum's (1973) cognitive–behavior modification. During eight 1-hr sessions conducted over 4 weeks, clients were trained to observe their cognitions and imagery during depressed moods. After clients were convinced of the links between their moods, thoughts, and images, they practiced cognitive restructuring skills for modifying their thoughts and images using imagery and positive self-statements (e.g., "I can see myself in the future coping with that particular situation"). Ten of eleven clients assigned to this condition completed it.

[12]In the religion-accommodative treatment, clients completed the same therapeutic protocol as that used in the standard treatment. The only difference is that participants were trained to replace their negative cogni-

tions and imagery with religious images (e.g., "I can visualize Christ going with me into that difficult situation in the future as I try to cope"). Seven of 9 clients assigned to this condition completed the treatment.

[13]*Pecheur & Edwards (1984).* Pecheur and Edwards (1984) assessed the differential efficacy of Beck et al.'s (1979) cognitive therapy for depression and a religion-accommodative version of the same therapy. Clients were students from a Christian college who met research diagnostic criteria for major depressive disorder. They also scored in the depressed range on the BDI, the Hamilton Rating Scale for Depression (HRSD; Hamilton, 1960), and a single-item visual analogue scale. In the standard treatment, clients completed eight 50-min sessions of cognitive behavior modification. All 7 clients who were assigned to this treatment completed it.

[14]In the religion-accommodative treatment, clients completed the standard cognitive therapy tasks specified in Beck et al. (1979); however, challenges to negative cognitions were placed in a religious context. For example, rather than replacing negative views of self with statements such as "Our self-acceptance and self-worth are not lost or lessened when we fail," the religion-accommodative approach trained clients to use self-statements such as, "God loves, accepts, and values us just as we are." This treatment was also administered according to a manual, which appears in Pecheur (1980).

[15]*Propst, Ostrom, Watkins, Dean, & Mashburn (1992).* Propst et al. (1992) compared the efficacy of Beck et al.'s (1979) cognitive therapy for depression with a manualized, religion-accommodative version of the same therapy (see Propst, 1988). Clients were recruited from the community and scored at least 14 on the 28-item version of the HRSD. They also scored at least in the moderate range on standard measures of religious commitment (e.g., Allport & Ross, 1967; King & Hunt, 1972). Clients in the standard treatment completed 18 sessions of individual cognitive therapy for depression. All 19 clients enrolled in this condition completed it.

[16]In the religion-accommodative treatment, clients completed 18 sessions of cognitive therapy that challenged negative cognitions and images by replacing them with positive thoughts and imagery of a religious nature, as in Propst (1980). All 19 clients enrolled in this condition completed it.

[17]*W. B. Johnson & Ridley (1992a).* W. B. Johnson and Ridley (1992a) compared the efficacy of rational-emotive therapy (RET), using Walen, DiGiuseppe, and Wessler's (1980) treatment manual, with a manualized, religion-accommodative version of the same therapy.

Clients were theology students and local church members who scored in at least the mildly depressed range on the BDI. They also scored in the "intrinsic" range on a standard measure of religious motivation (Allport & Ross, 1967), suggesting that their religious faith was highly internalized. In the standard RET condition, clients completed six 50-min sessions in 3 weeks, including homework sessions and in-session rehearsal of rational-emotive techniques. All 5 clients assigned to this condition completed it.

[18]In the religion-accommodative treatment, three explicitly Christian treatment components were added. First, clients were directed to dispute irrational beliefs using explicitly Christian beliefs, as in Propst (1980). Second, clients were encouraged to use Christian prayer, thoughts, and imagery in their homework assignments. Third, counselors used brief prayers at the end of each session. All 5 clients assigned to this condition completed it.

[19]W. B. Johnson et al. (1994). W. B. Johnson et al. (1994) compared the efficacy of standard RET and a religion-accommodative form of RET, as in W. B. Johnson and Ridley (1992a). Selection criteria were almost identical to those reported in W. B. Johnson and Ridley (1992a). The standard RET condition was an eight-session protocol delivered over 8 weeks, and was based on two popular RET treatment manuals (Ellis & Dryden, 1987; Walen et al., 1980). All 16 clients assigned to this condition completed it.

[20]The religion-accommodative treatment was based on two treatment manuals discussing Christian versions of RET (Backus, 1985; Thurman, 1989). Although the basic structure of RET was kept intact, clients were encouraged to dispute irrational beliefs based on scriptural beliefs and biblical examples. Homework assignments also used biblical examples and beliefs. All 16 clients assigned to this condition completed it.

Effect Size Estimates

[21]Effect sizes and homogeneity statistics were calculated from means and standard deviations using the DSTAT statistical software, Version 1.10 (B. T. Johnson, 1989), using the formulas prescribed by Hedges and Olkin (1985). Effect sizes were based on the difference between the mean of clients in the standard counseling condition and the mean of clients in the religion-accommodative conditions. This difference was divided by the pooled standard deviation of clients in both conditions. All effect size estimates, expressed as d_+ values, are corrected for the bias that is present in uncorrected g values, as recommended by Hedges and Olkin (1985).

Effect sizes can be interpreted as the increased amount of symptom reduction afforded to participants in the religion-accommodative condition, expressed in standard deviation units. In calculating aggregate effect size estimates, individual effect sizes were weighted by the inverse of their sampling error variance, so that studies with larger samples were given greater weight in the calculation of d_+ (Hedges & Olkin, 1985).

[22]The Q statistic was also used to estimate the degree of variability among the effect sizes. The Q statistic is basically a goodness-of-fit statistic with a roughly χ^2 distribution that enables a test of the hypothesis that all observed effect sizes were drawn from the same population. Significant Q values imply a heterogeneous set of effect sizes (Hunter & Schmidt, 1990).

Handling Multiple Dependent Measures

[23]All five studies used the BDI as a dependent measure of depression. Although two of the studies also used the HRSD or a single-item visual analogue measure of depression, or both (Pecheur & Edwards, 1984; Propst et al., 1992), effect size estimates were based exclusively on the BDI for three reasons. First, the BDI has been shown to produce conservative effect size estimates in comparison to rating scales that are completed by clinicians, such as the HRSD (Lambert, Hatch, Kingston, & Edwards, 1986). Second, single-item visual analogue measures of depression (e.g., Aitken, 1969) appear to contain remarkably little true score variance (Faravelli, Albanesi, & Poli, 1986). Third, the aggregation of data across multiple dependent measures requires knowing their intercorrelations, which were not available for all five studies. Thus, the individual and mean effect size estimates reported here can be considered to be somewhat conservative.

Handling Data from Multiple Follow-Up Periods

[24]All five studies collected follow-up data within 1 week of the termination of the trial. Although three of the studies (W. B. Johnson et al., 1994; Pecheur & Edwards, 1984; Propst et al., 1992) also reported follow-up data collected between 1 and 3 months after the termination of the trial, and one study (Propst et al., 1992) reported an effect size for a 24-month follow-up, we based our effect size estimates only on the data from the 1-week follow-up.

Other Problems with Coding Effect Sizes

[25]Some studies reported data on additional experimental conditions, including self-monitoring and therapist contact conditions (Propst, 1980), waiting list control conditions (Pecheur & Edwards, 1984; Propst et al.,

1992), and pastoral counseling conditions (Propst et al., 1992). Because none of these conditions were relevant to the central goal of this study, these data were neither coded nor included in the present meta-analytic study.

[26]Two other problems arose in coding effect sizes. First, although Propst (1980) reported posttreatment means on the BDI for both conditions, standard deviations were not reported. On the basis of the assumption that the other four studies in the present meta-analysis would yield similar pooled standard deviations for the BDI, a mean standard deviation for posttest scores on the BDI from these studies (5.81) was used as an imputed standard deviation for Propst (1980). This imputed standard deviation produced a nonsignificant test statistic for the comparison of the religious and standard counseling conditions, as Propst (1980) reported, giving us confidence that our imputed standard deviation was not wholly inaccurate.

[27]Second, Propst et al.'s (1992) results reported treatment effects separately for religious and nonreligious therapists, which was an independent factor in their experimental design. To collapse treatment effects across levels of the therapist religiousness factor, means and standard deviations obtained for religious and nonreligious therapists within each of the two religious counseling conditions were pooled before calculating an effect size for the treatments.

Corrections of Findings for Unreliability in Dependent Measures

[28]Scholars in meta-analysis advise that effect size estimates be corrected for biases (Hunter & Schmidt, 1990, 1994). One of the easiest biases to correct is attenuation resulting from unreliability in the dependent variable. This bias can be corrected by dividing observed effect sizes and standard errors by the square root of the internal consistency of the dependent variable. Because meta-analytic estimates of the BDI's internal consistency were readily available (Beck, Steer, & Garbin, 1988, estimated its internal consistency at $\alpha = .86$), the observed mean effect size and its confidence interval (CI) were divided by the square root of .86, or .927. Corrections for attenuation resulting from unreliability of the dependent variable produce increased effect size estimates but also a proportionate increase in confidence intervals; thus, a nonsignificant effect size will not become significant as a result of this correction (Hunter & Schmidt, 1994).

Estimating Clinical Significance

[29]We were also interested in whether religion-accommodative and standard approaches to counseling yielded clinically significant differences in efficacy (Jacobson & Revenstorf, 1988; Jacobson & Truax, 1991). Thus, we calculated meta-analytic summaries of clinical significance for two studies that reported clinical significance data (using BDI > 9 as a cutoff for "mild clinical depression"; Kendall, Hollon, Beck, Hammen, & Ingram, 1987).

Results

Observed Mean Effect Size and Attenuation-Corrected Effect Size

[30]The mean effect size for the difference between religious and standard counseling during the 1-week follow-up period (number of effect sizes = 5, $N = 111$) was $d_+ = +0.18$ (95% CI: −.20/+0.56), indicating that clients in religion-accommodative counseling had slightly lower BDI scores at 1-week follow-up than did clients in standard counseling conditions. This effect size was not reliably different from zero ($p = .34$). The five effect sizes that contributed to this mean effect size were homogeneous, $Q(4) = 5.38$, $p > .10$. The mean effect size after correcting the effects for attenuation resulting from unreliability was $d_+ = +0.20$ (95% CI: −0.19/+0.61).

Differences in Clinical Significance

[31]Two studies (W. B. Johnson & Ridley, 1992a; Propst, 1980) reported the percentage of participants in the religious and standard psychotherapy conditions who manifested evidence of at least mild clinical depression (BDI scores > 9) during the 1-week follow-up period. Aggregation of these data indicated that, among the 20 religion-accommodative counseling clients in the two studies, 4 (20%) were still at least mildly depressed at the end of treatment. Among the 26 standard counseling clients in the two studies, 9 (34.6%) were at least mildly depressed when treatment ended. This difference in clinical significance was not statistically significant, $\chi^2(1, N = 46) = 1.19$, $p > .10$.

Discussion

[32]The goal of the present study was to review the existing empirical evidence regarding the comparative efficacy of religion-accommodative approaches to counseling depressed religious clients. These data suggest that, in the immediate period after completion of counseling, religious approaches to counseling do not have any significant superiority to standard approaches to counseling. Given that the differences in efficacy of most bonafide treatments are surprisingly small (e.g., Lambert & Bergin, 1994; Wampold, 1997), the existing

literature on psychotherapy outcomes would have portended the present meta-analytic results. These findings corroborate some narrative reviews that claim equal efficacy for religion-accommodative and standard approaches to counseling (e.g., Worthington et al., 1996), and help to resolve the inconsistencies that others have observed among these studies (e.g., W. B. Johnson, 1993; Matthews et al., 1998).

[33]Although it is true that the religious approaches to counseling were no more effective than the standard approaches to counseling, it is equally true that they were no less effective than the standard approaches to counseling. Thus, the decision to use religion-accommodative approaches might be most wisely based not on the results of comparative clinical trials, which tend to find no differences among well-manualized treatments, but rather on the basis of patient choice (see Wampold, 1997). Not every religious client would prefer or respond favorably to a religion-accommodative approach to counseling. Indeed, the available evidence suggests that all but the most highly religious clients would prefer an approach to counseling that deals with religious issues only peripherally rather than focally (Wyatt & Johnson, 1990; see Worthington et al., 1996, for review).

[34]On the other hand, many religious clients—especially very conservative Christian clients—would indeed be attracted to a counseling approach (or counselor) precisely because the counseling approach (or the counselor) maintained that the clients' system of religious values were at the core of effective psychological change (Worthington et al., 1996). The research reviewed herein indicates that no empirical basis exists for withholding such religion-accommodative treatment from depressed religious clients who desire such a treatment approach.

The Last Word?

[35]There is inherent danger in publishing meta-analytic results. Because of their ability to provide precise-looking point estimates and short CIs (especially when the observed effect size estimates are relatively heterogeneous), meta-analytic summaries can be perceived to be the last word in evaluating research questions. It would be unfortunate if the present results were interpreted as the last word in evaluating the efficacy of religious approaches to counseling, however, because interesting and important questions remain.

[36]For example, although religion-accommodative approaches to counseling do not appear to be differentially efficacious in reducing symptoms (at least depres-

sive symptoms), they might produce differential treatment satisfaction among some religious clients. Also, comparative studies of religion-accommodative therapy are needed with longer follow-up periods. It is possible that religion-accommodative approaches might prove to be superior to standard treatments in longer term follow-up periods, particularly in helping clients from relapsing, for example, back into depressive episodes. The differential effects of religion-accommodative and standard approaches to treatment also need to be investigated for a wider variety of disorders, including anxiety, anger, alcohol and drug problems, and marital and family problems. As well, although religion-accommodative and standard approaches to counseling do not appear to influence clients' religiousness or religious values differentially (Worthington et al., 1996), it is possible that religion-accommodative counseling yields differential improvements in religious clients' spiritual well-being.

[37]Finally, on a technical note, it should be noted that the studies in this body of literature currently have been seriously underpowered (i.e., in all cases fewer than 20 clients per treatment). This literature would benefit enormously from as few as three or four very high-quality, large-sample (i.e., 30 or more clients per condition) studies that investigated these questions in greater detail. W. B. Johnson (1993) provided other helpful methodological recommendations to which research on religion-accommodative counseling should adhere.

Limitations

[38]The stability of meta-analytic findings comes from the number of studies included in the meta-analysis as well as the number of participants in the constituent studies. Thus, the findings from meta-analyses with small numbers of studies, such as the present study, are more easily overturned than meta-analyses that include larger numbers of studies. Although meta-analytic methods can be used to synthesize the results of as few as two studies (for examples of small-k meta-analyses, see Allison & Faith, 1996; Benschop et al., 1998; Kirsch, Montgomery, & Sapirstein, 1995; Uchino, Cacioppo, & Kiecolt-Glaser, 1996), our findings would obviously be considered more trustworthy if more studies had been available.

[39]A second limitation of the present findings relates to the nature of the meta-analytic sample. The five studies reviewed herein all investigated religion-accommodative counseling with depressed Christian clients. We can only speculate whether the present pattern of results would generalize to different religious

populations or to people with different sets of presenting problems. Obviously, research is needed to fill in such gaps.

Conclusion

[40]A variety of empirical data now suggest that certain forms of religious involvement can help prevent the onset of psychological difficulties and enhance effective coping with stressors. In addition, the majority of mental health professionals and the general public believe that patients' religious beliefs should be adequately assessed and taken into consideration in mental health treatment. Moreover, data indicate that patients' religious commitments can play a substantial role in counseling processes (Worthington et al., 1996). Data from the present study also indicate that religious approaches to counseling can be as effective as standard approaches to counseling depressed persons. Thus, for some clients, particularly very religious Christian clients, religion-accommodative approaches to counseling could be, quite literally, the treatment of choice. It is hoped that the present study will encourage counseling psychologists to examine whether religion-accommodative approaches yield similar or even superior benefits on other important metrics of therapeutic change and with other common difficulties in living.

References

Aitken, R. C. B. (1969). Measurement of feeling using visual analogue scales. *Proceedings of the Royal Society of Medicine, 62*, 989–993.

Allison, D. B., & Faith, M. S. (1996). Hypnosis as an adjunct to cognitive-behavioral psychotherapy for obesity: A meta-analytic reappraisal. *Journal of Consulting and Clinical Psychology, 64*, 513–516.

Allport, G. W., & Ross, J. M. (1967). Personal religious orientation and prejudice. *Journal of Personality and Social Psychology, 5*, 432–443.

Azhar, M. Z., & Varma, S. L. (1995a). Religious psychotherapy in depressive patients. *Psychotherapy and Psychosomatics, 63*, 165–168.

Azhar, M. Z., & Varma, S. L. (1995b). Religious psychotherapy as management of bereavement. *Acta Psychiatrica Scandinavica, 91*, 233–235.

Azhar, M. Z., Varma, S. L., & Dharap, A. S. (1994). Religious psychotherapy in anxiety disorder patients. *Acta Psychiatrica Scandinavica, 90*, 1–3.

Backus, W. (1985). *Telling the truth to troubled people.* Minneapolis, MN: Bethany House.

Beck, A. T. (1976). *Cognitive therapy and the emotional disorders.* New York: International University Press.

Beck, A. T., Rush, A. J., Shaw, B. F., & Emery, G. (1979). *Cognitive therapy of depression.* New York: Guilford Press.

Beck, A. T., Steer, R. A., & Garbin, M. G. (1988). Psychometric properties of the Beck Depression Inventory: Twenty-five years of evaluation. *Clinical Psychology Review, 8*, 77–100.

Beck, A. T., Ward, C. H., Mendelson, M., Mock, J. E., & Erbaugh, J. K. (1961). An inventory for measuring depression. *Archives of General Psychiatry, 4*, 561–571.

Benschop, R. J., Geenen, R., Mills, P. J., Naliboff, B. D., Kiecolt-Glaser, J. K., Herbert, T. B., van der Pompe, G., Miller, G., Matthews, K. A., Godaert, G. L. R., Gilmore, S. L., Glaser, R., Heijnen, C. J., Dopp, J. M., Bijlsma, J. W. J., Solomon, G. F., & Cacioppo, J. T. (1998). Cardiovascular and immune responses to acute psychological stress in young and old women: A meta-analysis. *Psychosomatic Medicine, 60*, 290–296.

Bergin, A. E. (1991). Values and religious issues in psychotherapy and mental health. *American Psychologist, 46*, 394–403.

Bergin, A. E., & Jensen, J. P. (1988). Mental health values of professional therapists: A national interdisciplinary survey. *Professional Psychology: Research and Practice, 19*, 290–297.

Bergin, A. E., Masters, K. S., & Richards, P. S. (1987). Religiousness and mental health reconsidered: A study of an intrinsically religious sample. *Journal of Counseling Psychology, 34*, 197–204.

Bienenfeld, D., Koenig, H. G., Larson, D. B., & Sherrill, K. A. (1997). Psychosocial predictors of mental health in a population of elderly women. *American Journal of Geriatric Psychiatry, 5*, 43–53.

Carlson, C. R., Bacaseta, P. E., & Simanton, D. A. (1988). A controlled evaluation of devotional meditation and progressive relaxation. *Journal of Psychology and Theology, 16*, 362–368.

Comstock, G. W., & Partridge, K. B. (1972). Church attendance and health. *Journal of Chronic Disease, 25*, 665–672.

Cooper, H., & Hedges, L. V. (1994). *Handbook of research synthesis.* New York: Russell Sage Foundation.

DeVries, R., Ridley, C. R., Pettorini, D., & Peterson, D. R. (1994). The comparative efficacy of Christian and secular rational-emotive therapy with Christian clients. *Journal of Psychology and Theology, 22*, 130–140.

Edwards, K. J. (1984). A comparison of secular and religious versions of cognitive therapy with depressed Christian college students. *Journal of Psychology and Theology, 12*, 45–54.

Ellis, A., & Dryden, W. (1987). *The practice of rational-emotive therapy.* New York: Springer.

Ellis, A., & Grieger, R. (1977). *Handbook of rational-emotive therapy.* New York: Springer.

Ellison, C. G. (1995). Race, religious involvement, and depressive symptomatology in a southeastern U.S. community. *Social Science and Medicine, 40*, 1561–1572.

Faravelli, C., Albanesi, G., & Poli, E. (1986). Assessment of depression: A comparison of rating scales. *Journal of Affective Disorders, 11*, 245–253.

Gallup, G. (1995). *The Gallup Poll: Public opinion 1995.* Wilmington, DE: Scholarly Resources.

Hamilton, M. (1960). A rating scale for depression. *Journal of Neurology, Neurosurgery, and Psychiatry, 23*, 56–62.

Hedges, L. V., & Olkin, I. (1985). *Statistical methods for meta-analysis.* Orlando, FL: Academic Press.

Houts, A. C., & Graham, K. (1986). Can religion make you crazy? Impact of client and therapist religious values on clinical judgments. *Journal of Consulting and Clinical Psychology, 54*, 267–271.

Hunter, J. E., & Schmidt, F. L. (1990). *Methods of meta-analysis: Correcting error and bias in research findings.* Newbury Park, CA: Sage.

Hunter, J. E., & Schmidt, F. L. (1994). Correcting for sources of artificial variation across studies. In H. Cooper & L. V. Hedges (Eds.), *Handbook of research synthesis* (pp. 323–336). New York: Russell Sage Foundation.

Jacobson, N. S., & Revenstorf, D. (1988). Statistics for assessing the clinical significance of psychotherapy techniques: Issues, problems, and new developments. *Behavioral Assessment, 10*, 133–145.

Jacobson, N. S., & Truax, P. (1991). Clinical significance: A statistical approach to defining meaningful change in psychotherapy research. *Journal of Consulting and Clinical Psychology, 59*, 12–19.

Johnson, B. T. (1989). *DSTAT: Software for the meta-analytic review of research literatures.* Hillsdale, NJ: Erlbaum.

Johnson, W. B. (1991). *The comparative efficacy of religious and nonreligious rational-emotive therapy with religious clients.* Unpublished doctoral dissertation, Fuller Graduate School of Psychology, Pasadena, CA.

Johnson, W. B. (1993). Outcome research and religious psychotherapies: Where are we and where are we going? *Journal of Psychology and Theology, 21*, 297–308.

Johnson, W. B., & Ridley, C. R. (1992b). Sources of gain in Christian counseling and psychotherapy. *The Counseling Psychologist, 20*, 159–175.

Kark, J. D., Shemi, G., Friedlander, Y., Martin, O., Manor, O., & Blondheim, S. H. (1996). Does religious observance promote health? Mortality in secular vs. religious kibbutzim in Israel. *American Journal of Public Health, 86*, 341–346.

Kelly, E. W. (1995). Counselor values: A national survey. *Journal of Counseling and Development, 73*, 648–653.

Kelly, T. A., & Strupp, H. H. (1992). Patient and therapist values in psychotherapy: Perceived changes, assimilation, similarity, and outcome. *Journal of Consulting and Clinical Psychology, 60*, 34–40.

Kendall, P. C., Hollon, S. D., Beck, A. T., Hammen, C. L., & Ingram, R. E. (1987). Issues and recommendations regarding use of the Beck Depression Inventory. *Cognitive Therapy and Research, 11*, 289–299.

Kendler, K. S., Gardner, C. O., & Prescott, C. A. (1997). Religion, psychopathology, and substance use and abuse: A multimeasure, genetic-epidemiologic study. *American Journal of Psychiatry, 154*, 322–329.

King, M. A., & Hunt, R. A. (1972). Measuring the religious variable: A replication. *Journal for the Scientific Study of Religion, 11*, 240–251.

Kirsch, I., Montgomery, G., & Sapirstein, G. (1995). Hypnosis as an adjunct to cognitive-behavioral psychotherapy: A meta-analysis. *Journal of Consulting and Clinical Psychology, 63*, 214–220.

Koenig, H. G., George, L. K., & Peterson, B. L. (1998). Religiosity and remission of depression in medically ill older patients. *American Journal of Psychiatry, 155*, 536–542.

Kosmin, B. A., & Lachman, S. P. (1993). *One nation under God: Religion in contemporary American society.* New York: Harmony.

Lambert, M. J., & Bergin, A. E. (1994). The effectiveness of psychotherapy. In A. E. Bergin & S. L. Garfield (Eds.), *Handbook of psychotherapy and behavior change*

(4th ed., pp. 143–189). New York: Wiley.

Lambert, M. J., Hatch, D. R., Kingston, M. D., & Edwards, B. C. (1986). Zung, Beck, and Hamilton rating scales as measures of treatment outcome: A meta-analytic comparison. *Journal of Consulting and Clinical Psychology, 54*, 54–59.

Larson, D. B., Sherrill, K. A., Lyons, J. S., Craigie, F. C., Thielman, S. B., Greenwold, M. A., & Larson, S. S. (1992). Associations between dimensions of religious commitment and mental health reported in the *American Journal of Psychiatry* and *Archives of General Psychiatry*: 1978–1989. *American Journal of Psychiatry, 149*, 557–559.

Lewis, K. N., & Lewis, D. A. (1985). Impact of religious affiliation on therapists' judgments of patients. *Journal of Consulting and Clinical Psychology, 53*, 926–932.

Luborsky, L., Mintz, J., Auerbach, A., Cristoph, P., Bachrach, H., Todd, T., Johnson, M., Cohen, M., & O'Brien, C. P. (1980). Predicting the outcome of psychotherapy: Findings of the Penn Psychotherapy Project. *Archives of General Psychiatry, 37*, 471–481.

Matthews, D. A., McCullough, M. E., Larson, D. B., Koenig, H. G., Swyers, J. P., & Milano, M. G. (1998). Religious commitment and health: A review of the research and implications for family medicine. *Archives of Family Medicine, 7*, 118–124.

McCullough, M. E., & Worthington, E. L. (1995). College students' perceptions of a psychotherapist's treatment of a religious issue: Partial replication and extension. *Journal of Counseling and Development, 73*, 626–634.

McCullough, M. E., Worthington, E. L., Maxey, J., & Rachal, K. C. (1997). Gender in the context of supportive and challenging religious counseling interventions. *Journal of Counseling Psychology, 44*, 80–88.

Meichenbaum, D. (1973). *Therapist manual for cognitive behavior modification*. Unpublished manuscript, University of Waterloo, Ontario, Canada.

Meichenbaum, D. (1985). *Stress inoculation training*. New York: Pergamon Press.

Miller, L., Warner, V., Wickramaratne, P., & Weissman, M. (1997). Religiosity and depression: Ten-year follow-up of depressed mothers and offspring. *Journal of the American Academy of Child and Adolescent Psychiatry, 36*, 1416–1425.

Morrow, D., Worthington, E. L., & McCullough, M. E. (1993). Observers' perceptions of a psychotherapist's treatment of a religious issue. *Journal of Counseling and Development, 71*, 452–456.

Neeleman, J., & King, M. B. (1993). Psychiatrists' religious attitudes in relation to their clinical practice: A survey of 231 psychiatrists. *Acta Psychiatrica Scandinavica, 88*, 420–424.

Ostrom, R., Watkins, P., Dean, T., & Mashburn, D. (1992). Comparative efficacy of religious and nonreligious cognitive-behavioral therapy for the treatment of clinical depression in religious individuals. *Journal of Consulting and Clinical Psychology, 60*, 94–103.

Pargament, K. I. (1997). *The psychology of religion and coping*. New York: Guilford Press.

Pargament, K. I., Ensing, D. S., Falgout, K., Olsen, H., Reilly, B., Van Haitsma, K., & Warren, R. (1990). God help me: I. Religious coping efforts as predictors of the outcomes to significant life events. *American Journal of Community Psychology, 18*, 793–824.

Pargament, K. I., Ishler, K., Dubow, E., Stanik, P., Rouiller, R., Crowe, P., Cullman, E., Albert, M., & Royster, B. J. (1994). Methods of religious coping with the Gulf War: Cross-sectional and longitudinal analyses. *Journal for the Scientific Study of Religion, 33*, 347–361.

Pargament, K. I., Smith, B., & Brant, C. (1995, November). *Religious and nonreligious coping methods with the 1993 Midwest flood*. Paper presented at the meeting of the Society for the Scientific Study of Religion, St. Louis, MO.

Payne, I. R., Bergin, A. E., & Loftus, P. E. (1992). A review of attempts to integrate spiritual and standard psychotherapy techniques. *Journal of Psychotherapy Integration, 2*, 171–192.

Pecheur, D. (1980). *A comparison of the efficacy of secular and religious cognitive behavior modification in the treatment of depressed Christian college students*. Unpublished doctoral dissertation, Rosemead School of Psychology, La Mirada, CA.

Propst, R. L. (1980). The comparative efficacy of religious and nonreligious imagery for the treatment of mild depression in religious individuals. *Cognitive Therapy and Research, 4*, 167–178.

Propst, R. L. (1988). *Psychotherapy in a religious framework*. New York: Human Sciences Press.

Propst, R. L. (1996). Cognitive-behavioral therapy and the religious person. In E. P. Shafranske (Ed.), *Religion in the clinical practice of psychology* (pp. 391–408). Washington, DC: American Psychological Association.

Richards, P. S., & Bergin, A. E. (1997). *A spiritual strategy for counseling and psychotherapy*. Washington, DC: American Psychological Association.

Richards, P. S., Owen, L., & Stein, S. (1993). A religiously oriented group counseling intervention for self-defeating perfectionism: A pilot study. *Counseling and Values, 37*, 96–104.

Ridley, C. R. (1992a). Brief Christian and non-Christian rational-emotive therapy with depressed Christian clients: An exploratory study. *Counseling and Values, 36*, 220–229.

Rye, M. S., & Pargament, K. I. (1997, August). *Forgiveness and romantic relationships in college*. Paper presented at the 105th Annual Convention of the American Psychological Association, Chicago.

Schumaker, J. F. (1992). *Religion and mental health*. New York: Oxford University Press.

Shafranske, E. P. (1996). *Religion and the clinical practice of psychology*. Washington, DC: American Psychological Association.

Shafranske, E. P., & Malony, H. N. (1990). Clinical psychologists' religious and spiritual orientations and their practice of psychotherapy. *Psychotherapy, 27*, 72–78.

Thurman, C. (1989). *The lies we believe*. Nashville, TN: Thomas Nelson.

Toh, Y., & Tan, S. Y. (1997). The effectiveness of church-based lay counselors: A controlled outcome study. *Journal of Psychology and Christianity, 16*, 260–267.

Uchino, B. N., Cacioppo, J. T., & Kiecolt-Glaser, J. K. (1996). The relationship between social support and physiological processes: A review with emphasis on underlying mechanisms and implications for health. *Psychological Bulletin, 119*, 488–531.

Walen, S. R., DiGiuseppe, R., & Wessler, R. (1980). *A practitioner's guide to rational emotive therapy*. New York: Oxford University Press.

Wampold, B. E. (1997). Methodological problems in identifying efficacious psychotherapies. *Psychotherapy Research, 7*, 21–43.

Wandrei, K. E. (1985). Identifying potential suicides among high-risk women. *Social Work, 30*, 511–517.

Worthington, E. L., Kurusu, T. A., McCullough, M. E., & Sandage, S. J. (1996). Empirical research on religion and psychotherapeutic processes and outcomes: A ten-year review and research prospectus. *Psychological Bulletin, 119*, 448–487.

Wyatt, S. C., & Johnson, R. W. (1990). The influence of counselors' religious values on clients' perceptions of the counselor. *Journal of Psychology and Theology, 18*, 158–165.

Address correspondence to: Michael E. McCullough, National Institute for Healthcare Research, 6110 Executive Boulevard, Suite 908, Rockville, MD 20852. Electronic mail may be sent to Mike@nihr.org

From *Journal of Counseling Psychology, 46*, 92–98. Copyright © 1999 by the American Psychological Association, Inc. Reprinted with permission.

Discussion Questions for Model Literature Review 3

Editorial note: All the sample literature reviews in this book are presented as strong models. However, there are differences of opinion on the effectiveness of any particular piece of writing, even among experts. While answering the following questions, consider the guidelines in this book (as *only* guidelines, not principles) as well as your own standards for effective writing.

1. Briefly comment on the adequacy of the title of the review.

2. Comment on the adequacy of the Abstract, if any. Does it effectively summarize the essence of the review given that abstracts are restricted to 120 words or less in the journal in which this review article appeared?

3. Does the review have a strong beginning? Does it get straight to the point? If not, has the author used some other effective technique to begin the review?

4. Has the author made a strong case for reviewing the topic(s) he covered? Has the author shown that the topic(s) are important?

5. Is the material presented in a logical sequence? Are the headings (and subheadings, if any) appropriate and helpful?

6. Are key variables adequately defined? Are they defined at appropriate points? Explain.

7. Are there points where the references are not well integrated with each other (i.e., simply described as an annotated list)? Explain.

8. Are the strengths and weaknesses of some of the cited research described? If yes, name at least one section where this is done using paragraph numbers.

9. Has the author made it clear what material is his and what is being summarized/paraphrased from other sources? Explain.

10. Are any portions of the review unclear to you? If so, identify them by paragraph number(s).

11. Are the individual paragraphs straightforward and to the point? Explain. If yes, identify one by number that you think is especially good. If no, identify one that is weak.

12. Is the conclusion/discussion at the end of the review appropriate in light of the material covered earlier?

13. On a scale from 1 (very weak) to 10 (very strong), what is your overall evaluation of the literature review? Name one or two considerations that strongly influenced your evaluation.

14. Assume that you are on the editorial board of an academic journal and that the general topic of this review is within the scope of what the journal usually publishes. Which of the following would you recommend to the editor of the journal: publish as is, publish only after minor revisions, publish only after major revisions, *or* do not publish? Briefly defend your recommendation.

Table 1

Table of z-Values for r

r	z	r	z	r	z	r	z	r	z
.000	.000	.200	.203	.400	.424	.600	.693	.800	1.099
.005	.005	.205	.208	.405	.430	.605	.701	.805	1.113
.010	.010	.210	.213	.410	.436	.610	.709	.810	1.127
.015	.015	.215	.218	.415	.442	.615	.717	.815	1.142
.020	.020	.220	.224	.420	.448	.620	.725	.820	1.157
.025	.025	.225	.229	.425	.454	.625	.733	.825	1.172
.030	.030	.230	.234	.430	.460	.630	.741	.830	1.188
.035	.035	.235	.239	.435	.466	.635	.750	.835	1.204
.040	.040	.240	.245	.440	.472	.640	.758	.840	1.221
.045	.045	.245	.250	.445	.478	.645	.767	.845	1.238
.050	.050	.250	.255	.450	.485	.650	.775	.850	1.256
.055	.055	.255	.261	.455	.491	.655	.784	.855	1.274
.060	.060	.260	.266	.460	.497	.660	.793	.860	1.293
.065	.065	.265	.271	.465	.504	.665	.802	.865	1.313
.070	.070	.270	.277	.470	.510	.670	.811	.870	1.333
.075	.075	.275	.282	.475	.517	.675	.820	.875	1.354
.080	.080	.280	.288	.480	.523	.680	.829	.880	1.376
.085	.085	.285	.293	.485	.530	.685	.838	.885	1.398
.090	.090	.290	.299	.490	.536	.690	.848	.890	1.422
.095	.095	.295	.304	.495	.543	.695	.858	.895	1.447
.100	.100	.300	.310	.500	.549	.700	.867	.900	1.472
.105	.105	.305	.315	.505	.556	.705	.877	.905	1.499
.110	.110	.310	.321	.510	.563	.710	.887	.910	1.528
.115	.116	.315	.326	.515	.570	.715	.897	.915	1.557
.120	.121	.320	.332	.520	.576	.720	.908	.920	1.589
.125	.126	.325	.337	.525	.583	.725	.918	.925	1.623
.130	.131	.330	.343	.530	.590	.730	.929	.930	1.658
.135	.136	.335	.348	.535	.597	.735	.940	.935	1.697
.140	.141	.340	.354	.540	.604	.740	.950	.940	1.738
.145	.146	.345	.360	.545	.611	.745	.962	.945	1.783
.150	.151	.350	.365	.550	.618	.750	.973	.950	1.832
.155	.156	.355	.371	.555	.626	.755	.984	.955	1.886
.160	.161	.360	.377	.560	.633	.760	.996	.960	1.946
.165	.167	.365	.383	.565	.640	.765	1.008	.965	2.014
.170	.172	.370	.388	.570	.648	.770	1.020	.970	2.092
.175	.177	.375	.394	.575	.655	.775	1.033	.975	2.185
.180	.182	.380	.400	.580	.662	.780	1.045	.980	2.298
.185	.187	.385	.406	.585	.670	.785	1.058	.985	2.443
.190	.192	.390	.412	.590	.678	.790	1.071	.990	2.647
.195	.198	.395	.418	.595	.685	.795	1.085	.995	2.994

Table 2

Table for Converting Cohen's *d* to *r*

Cohen's *d*	Correlation Coefficient *r*
2.0	.707
1.9	.689
1.8	.669
1.7	.648
1.6	.625
1.5	.600
1.4	.573
1.3	.545
1.2	.514
1.1	.482
1.0	.447
0.9	.410
0.8	.371
0.7	.330
0.6	.287
0.5	.243
0.4	.196
0.3	.148
0.2	.100
0.1	.050
0.0	.000